JESSICA MARRIOTT & DR. BLUMA SAPIR

I'M RIGHT, YOU'RE STUPID

GROWING UP YOUR SIBLING RELATIONSHIP

PUBLISHED BY ROOTS READS

www.yoursibhub.com

Copyright © 2025 Jessica Marriott and Dr. Bluma Sapir.

All rights reserved under International and
Pan-American Copyright Conventions.

No part of this book may be reproduced in any form or by any electronic or mechanical means, including information storage and retrieval systems, without permission in writing from the publisher, except by a reviewer, who may quote brief passages in a review. No part of this book may be used or reproduced in any manner for the purpose of training artificial intelligence technologies or systems, without permission in writing from the publisher.

First Edition

Hardcover ISBN: 979-8-218-73163-2
Paperback ISBN: 979-8-9931742-7-3
eBook ISBN: 979-8-9931742-6-6
Audiobook ISBN: 79-8-9931742-5-9

Roots Reads, an imprint of SibHub LLC
3625 N Bishop Lane, Scottsdale, AZ. 85251

Dedication

For every sibling carrying the weight of their past or the past they inherited,—may love, understanding, and healing rewrite your story creating a brighter future together.

Acknowledgements

Despite our unwavering obedience to this mission, publishing our book took a village. We are deeply grateful to those who have surrounded us with love, wisdom, and support, offered grounding encouragement, celebrated moments of joy, and stood by us through the various challenges we faced along our journey. We are grateful for your steadfast presence, which has been woven into every page of this book, leaving an indelible imprint. This work reflects the light you shined upon us, that sustained us, and served as guideposts along the way. Thank you, thank you, thank you.

To our family: Mom & Joe, Dad, Sara and Adam, Jon, Liv, Shmu, Esther, Gabe, Tuvia, and Cobi; Aunt Susie, Uncle Arny, Uncle Richy & Auntie Donna.

To our friends: Steve K, Edgar P, Lisette & Carlos, Louise, Kim H, Crystal L, Kasey V, Susie M, Jono W, Jen A, Doug S, Kathleen T, Mary K, Becky C-V, Dannielle V, Lauren F.

To our mentors: Drs. Chuck Garcia, Laurie Kramer, Ronald Rohner, Winnie Dunn, Nadia Brusweiler-Stern, Frances Champagne, C.Sue Carter, Stephen Porges, Wayne Dyer, John & Julie Gottman, Sue Johnson, Esther Perel, David Tong, Brian

Greene; Ms. Jacqueline Spier, Ms. Lee Schwartz, and the one and only Tony Robbins.

To our contributors: Steve Kaplowitz, Edgar Pablos, Chris Hanna and team, Steve Carlis and team, Meaghan Beatley, Lindsay Rayball, Noam Shumack and the JCC-Miami Beach, R'Ben Zeidman and Temple Mt. Siani, Zoom Founder Eric Yuan, Cannes World Film Festival, Texas Short Film Festival (Mikel Fair), Culver City Film Festival (Peter Greene), Mesa International Film Festival, Silicon Beach Film Festival (Peter Greene), Oregon Short Film Festival (Mike Fair), Nevada Women's Film Festival (Kelsie Stacy), El Paso Media Fest (Chris Hanna).

May we all live abundantly and authentically, connected, whole and united.

Contents

Dedication iii

Acknowledgements v

Introduction 1

Chapter 1: Our Story 7

Chapter 2: Why You Need To Heal Your Sibling Relationship 25

Chapter 3: How Your Parents Affect Your Sibling Relationship 49

Chapter 4: How Your Sibling Relationship Affects You And Your Future Relationships 75

Chapter 5: Getting Started: Emotional Regulation 89

THE 6 STEPS TO HEALING: 101

Chapter 6: Step 1 - Create A New Contract 103

Chapter 7: Step 2 - Identify Your Archetypes 111

Chapter 8: Step 3 - Memory Sharing 123

Chapter 9: Step 4 - Learning To Move Through Conflict..................147

Chapter 10: Step 5 - Cultural Fusion...167

Chapter 11: Step 6 - Managing Your Evolution
(Wash, Rinse, Repeat)..181

Chapter 12: Conclusion...197

Introduction

If we had to choose one word to describe our childhood, it would be chaos. We grew up during the '70s and '80s, when most parents ushered their toddlers out of the house to run wild around town unsupervised and didn't mind their teens hitchhiking to school or concerts. This was a brief window of time when families rejected the structured *Leave it to Beaver*-style parenting of the 50s and 60s, right before the "stranger danger" panic of the '90s put a definite end to this free-for-all. That was the baseline for all of our friends and neighbors. But our family took it to another extreme.

We had loose boundaries growing up, either because there were no limits, or the ones our parents gave us were ignored. We snuck out cars before our feet could reach the pedals. We got high before *Shabbat* (Sabbath), barely holding back our laughter at the dinner table. We hopped the border - our literal backyard fence as El Paso natives - to Mexico to party in "Drink and Drowns" that would put *The Hangover* to shame. Jessica made out with a *Scarface* movie star a few feet away from the original Wonder Woman, Linda Carter, before she turned 17.

We were like a pair of race cars hurtling down an ever-stretching open road; a nuclear chain reaction in full swing. That kind of energy can be beautiful. It bonded us as sisters. We had to have each other's back to survive. When a classmate threatened to beat up Bluma, she didn't hesitate to turn to Jessica, who swiftly went to find the classmate and take her down, losing a sneaker in the scuffle. Bluma still owes Jessica a shoe.

But too much chaos risks destroying the good it creates. Because our parents weren't very present in our lives as young children, we craved their attention. We desperately wanted to feel their presence and to feel accepted by them. We yearned for them like sunflowers stretching their necks out to the sun. But since there was a limited supply of that attention, we unconsciously felt like we had to compete against each other to obtain it. Too often, this resulted in explosive fights. And we mean explosive - screaming, crying, scratching and punching. These were fights that left us feeling shattered and fuming, the aftermath of which hung over us like a cloud of toxic smoke, ready to engulf us again with the next outburst. We didn't know how to disagree without fighting or how to make up after. No one taught us that there is a healthy way to fight/argue. No adult - no parent, grandparent or teacher - ever intervened constructively. The more we fought, the more venomous we felt towards each other. Over time, a childhood dynamic of verbal and physical attacks turned into emotional abuse between us. We grew to resent each other so deeply that by the time we were adults, we were basically estranged. We

INTRODUCTION

thought we were better off without each other. It took us half of our lives to realize how incredibly, deeply mistaken we were.

The truth is that your sibling dynamic impacts every other part of your life. But we didn't know that. Most of us aren't conscious of it. We didn't realize how our wild childhood and the antagonism it bred between us made us feel anxious, unseen and unloved as children and teenagers, and not just by each other. Sibling relationships are the bedrock on which all other relationships are founded: we attract and are attracted to people who remind us of them. This is attachment theory, and we'll get a whole lot more into it in Chapter 3. The point is that we didn't see how the anxiety and lack of understanding we felt with each other, at an unconscious level, also followed us - haunted us - well into adulthood, impacting our relationships with other people beyond our original family circle.

Until finally, after a lot of soul-searching, we got it. We came to understand that our hostile sibling dynamic was what was holding us back from reaching our full potential as individuals and as siblings. It was the biggest wake-up call of our lives. Someone once told us, "If you don't get it right in your nuclear family, you don't get it right."[1] It's 100% true.

So one day in November 2019 - mere weeks before the Covid-19 pandemic engulfed the globe and changed life as we know it - we decided to do something crazy. Something even wilder than our feral childhood. We decided to grab the bull by the horns and fix our broken relationship. Before "zoom" had even become a verb people casually threw around, we looked

---

[1] "Roots Tour" documentary.

at each other through our phone screens from across the world and made each other a promise: we would bridge the gap that had separated us for too long. We would be those feisty teens who stopped at nothing to protect each other, even if it meant losing a shoe. We would unite.

This was totally new for us. After years of repressing memories from our chaotic past, we suddenly dove right into them. We unwrapped ourselves, exposing our very cores, wounds and all, to each other, the very people who had terrorized us growing up. We didn't even know if we'd succeed. It was a total and utter l...e...a...p of faith.

Chances are you have felt or are feeling the same way about your sibling, or you know someone who is, or you are thinking of your children's relationship with each other. You may be fighting, have recently fallen out, or been estranged for years. You probably think your sibling is difficult and unreasonable - impossible, even - and they feel the same about you. You might have given up on the hope or possibility of ever feeling close to them, of seeing them as an ally and friend.

We get it.

For almost half of our lives, that's how we felt about each other. But we're here to tell you that it can change. Our tentative leap of faith not only paid off; it transformed our lives. Today we are sisters in the true sense of the word - not mere biological inmates sharing the same genetic makeup.

We are two humans whose past, present and future are intertwined. When one of us experiences joy or sorrow, the other shares in it. Becoming loving, supportive siblings has unlocked a trove of peace, happiness and potential we hadn't even known we were missing. It's as if we'd been going through life with our right arm in a sling, struggling to accomplish daily tasks with our left hand only. Then one day the sling fell off and we realized we had this whole other limb at our disposal. Everything was suddenly so much easier to manage. Our movements were more graceful. We were whole.

We want you to be whole, too. We want you to be unburdened by the negative energy and strife holding you back. We want you to live up to your full potential and feel the miraculous love and joy we now feel as reunited siblings.

We are excited and grateful to join you on this journey, and for you to become part of our family. We can't wait for you to feel full of love and at one with the universe. To come out on the other side. Stronger. Wiser. And United.

CHAPTER 1

Our Story

Let's start at the beginning. Our parents, a former schoolteacher and a radio station owner, decided to settle down in El Paso, Texas, and start a family. Jessica was the first of us four siblings to come into the world. She was a curious and active child, and, three years later when Bluma Claire was born, she was delighted at having a baby sister. She was so thrilled, in fact, that one evening, while our parents entertained guests in the living room, she pulled baby Bluma out of her crib and carried her into the living room, bucking under the weight, to show her off. Our mom, panicking at the sight of her infant dangling in the arms of her toddler, quickly rescued Bluma and scolded Jessica.

This is a bittersweet story, and one of the earliest examples of a narrative that will come to define us as sisters. You'll see why soon.

Though we shared the same sense of curiosity and adventure, we were in other fundamental ways very different children. Bluma had a gift for words. By the time she was two, she knew all the words to songs. She could read people very easily and give the kind of advice an emotional coach would give their clients, except she was a child. Our mom, who was also a wordsmith but didn't always have the confidence to speak her mind, admired Bluma for her ability to think and speak simultaneously with the ease of a seasoned public speaker.

Jessica, on the other hand, was a natural-born athlete. She was both physically strong and dexterous, and had an iron will to push herself beyond her limits. That same willpower helped her cope with a diagnosis that would shape the rest of her life. After struggling throughout first grade, Jessica was diagnosed with dyslexia in second grade, which she had to repeat. Our dad, who is also dyslexic, identified with Jessica and her struggle, and this bound them in a particular way.

So from an early age, Bluma communicated best with words and was closest to our mom, while Jessica best manifested through actions and more easily related with our dad. These differences didn't have to create a rift. Yet, by the time Bluma was four and Jessica was seven, we were constantly at each other's throats.

Why? Well, it's taken us a lifetime to understand this, and that's what we explore in this book. There are many interconnected and complex reasons that we'll dissect in the following chapters. Here's part of it: the natural differences between us - the stuff that feeds normal and healthy sibling rivalry - bumped up against the way each of our parents treated us differently - due to their own complicated family histories and the ways they projected these onto us - and created a combative framework in which we felt like we had to compete against each other for our parents' affection, and then lash out at each other when we felt like we weren't able to obtain this.

Jessica, a preternaturally curious child, loved learning, but her dyslexia made schoolwork an excruciating endeavor. She tortured herself and our mother, who felt compelled to spend hours every night helping Jessica just to finish her homework. Bluma, on the other hand, didn't struggle in this way, and so was carefree when it came to school. She rarely got on top of her homework and hardly studied for tests, but still managed to sail through class and obtain decent grades. Jessica resented Bluma for not even trying while she worked three times harder.

Meanwhile, Bluma, a curvy teen with curly hair, was jealous of Jessica, who was petite with sleek brown hair. From the time Jessica was 10, our father encouraged her to stand in front of the mirror and repeat to herself, "I'm beautiful," as a self-esteem building mantra. However, when Bluma announced she wanted to pursue acting, our dad told her, "There's a lot of rejection in acting, so I'm going to tell you this so it doesn't hurt as much when *other* people tell you: You're not beautiful." The flawed, polarizing message was clear: Bluma had the brains and Jessica had the beauty. It was deeply hurtful to hear. And of course, it wasn't true. We're both beautiful and bright. We all are. You are, too.

So, we both carried around a deep well of frustration and didn't know how to resolve it. We didn't have role models to show us how. Our parents did the best they could at the time, and we love them for that. We know how hard and exhausting parenting is, and we give them all the grace in the world. They simply couldn't teach us what they themselves did not know.

Our dad worked nonstop so we hardly saw him, but when we did, he would be in one of three moods. He could be a ray of sunshine with an infectious energy that could get you excited about anything. Or he could be a zoned-out TV watcher, planted on the living room sofa, eating and watching movies before falling asleep. Or, he could be a bully. He was often angry and impatient and would lash out at us, demeaning us with his words and occasionally resorting to more physical forms of violence. So we learned three speeds too: to have fun, to withdraw or to lash out.

Our mother, on the other hand, was quiet and conflict averse. Along with keeping our family afloat, she would busy herself with volunteer work. She simply didn't have the bandwidth to arbitrate conflicts at home. Like many moms, she would tune out our bickering until it had escalated past the point of no return, at which point, she'd invariably take Bluma's side. She wasn't conscious of playing favorites, but that's what it felt like, and it made us resent each other even more.

So we fought. All the time.

We had different weapons. Generally, Bluma used her words. She knew exactly what to say to make Jessica feel less than, stupid and unvalued. Jessica fought with her fists, which was painful and demoralizing for Bluma, leaving scars on her body and creating a hypervigilance toward future attacks long after they ended. Our lives together were a round-robin of fighting. Many of our brawls stemmed from some kind of feeling of sibling injustice, where we both felt like we had to defend ourselves. Bluma would react to something Jessica did, or vice versa. But over time, our fights turned into something uglier. We became each other's punching bags, spewing hate at each other for reasons that had nothing to do with each other directly. A bad day at school. An argument with a friend. That was enough for Jessica to punch, scratch, or slap Bluma, and for Bluma to say something to Jessica she knew would leave her feeling like an open wound.

Of course, we had our moments of closeness. We've already told you about Jessica losing a shoe to defend Bluma when another girl threatened to beat her up. There was also the time in youth group when our Rabbi told us to team up and come up with a plan in case our parents died and we had to provide for ourselves. (We think the point was to teach us resilience and reliability). We immediately latched on to each other and roared with laughter as we came up with our own outrageous plan. We'd become "entrepreneurs" and sell drugs, and if we got caught, we'd go to jail and in that way obtain shelter and food. That's what we said, straight-faced, to an assembly of kids who'd just walked us through their business or charity ideas. In these rare moments, we were peas in a pod.

These brief flickers of truce felt amazing. But the next blowout felt all the more devastating as a result. Our whole relationship felt like walking on eggshells.

Ultimately, when we left home for college, we wanted out of the chaos that had marked our childhood. We got to focus on things that were important to us and grow as individuals. Bluma's innate ability to see the root cause of a problem, perceive resistance, and find a way through it, paved the way for her successful career as a clinical psychologist. Jessica, the eternal striver and life learner, always seeking out a new challenge, became an entrepreneur. When we did see each other, during holidays with our family, we tolerated one another, though barely - every encounter ended with verbal blows and emotional upheaval. And our mom would reinforce this dynamic, picking sides with Bluma. So, we chose to forge ahead without each other. We fell in love, married, and had children, forming parallel lives.

By 2013, we were more or less estranged. Then Jessica got sick. As an entrepreneur and a marathon runner, Jessica loved motion. She was always on her feet, dashing around to finish a race or finalize a deal. But for reasons doctors could never fully diagnose, something attacked her joints, tendons and muscles. What started out as pain in her finger soon took over her whole body, immobilizing her. She could barely stand, or walk. The slightest movement or touch was astoundingly painful. Even the embrace of her 8-year-old twins felt like it could break her. It was a terrifying experience, and she found herself facing it largely on her own. At this point, she was living in Scottsdale. Just as our mother committed to helping Jessica's learning issues, she dove into helping Jessica come up with a game plan on how to help her heal. Jessica fought tooth and nail to gain strength and tried every therapy.

While seeking out a remedy, cycling through doctors and naturopaths, a friend suggested she start keeping a journal. Jessica, at first, rejected the idea. Journaling was something Bluma had always done and used against her; Bluma had poured her heart out into her journals and recorded our fights with pristine detail, referring back to them to supply our mom with evidence of Jessica's wrongdoing. Jessica had had no such tool. Growing up, she'd never sat still long enough to listen to her feelings and name them, much less write them down. It wasn't something that had come naturally to her.

But after several weeks at home, Jessica took up pen and paper and started writing. Feeling the pain surge through her body compelled her to think back on other painful moments in her life. Her childhood - her constant fighting with Bluma - stood out prominently. Her thoughts circled around the feelings of hurt, alienation and rejection from our mom siding with Bluma. And now, she had all the time in the world to sit with these thoughts and write them down.

She was also a different person. She was a mother. She could look back at her past from two vantage points: that of the child she'd been, but also the mom she was now. Jessica understood how tough it must have been for our mom to raise us and gave her grace. But she realized there was another way to raise children without fueling hostility between them. As her body slowly, eventually healed, gaining her strength and mobility back, she wrote. A stream of words led her to an epiphany. What she and Bluma had experienced growing up was not healthy. They'd grown up in an abusive household. But not only in a traditional or conventional sense, where a parent harms their child - Bluma had been Jessica's tormentor, and Jessica had been Bluma's oppressor. What we had experienced was sibling abuse.

This, she knew, was a defining aspect of her life. Jessica believed heart and soul in the tenets of self-improvement. She's read hundreds of books, and for 10 years had studied and taught

Dale Carnegie, the author of *How to Win Friends and Influence People* who is widely considered the father of self-improvement.

It had changed her as a person. From our upbringing, we learned to be cautious of other people who could take advantage of us. Carnegie's teachings showed Jessica how to be a compassionate person - interested in others while maintaining good boundaries. She had become a better person as a result. But for all the hard work she'd done on herself personally, the mere thought of Bluma sent her straight back to childhood and the sense of impotent rage she'd carried inside her. She was stuck there. And now she knew why. She wanted to tell Bluma, but she didn't know how.

Jessica started with an email, tentatively broaching the pain from their past, and imparting a glimpse into the growth she was experiencing. Bluma saw the email in her inbox, drew in a deep breath and opened it. She saw a long message with quotes from books Jessica was reading. Bluma instantly closed the message. She was averse to Jessica's know-it-all swagger. She felt that for all of Jessica's years with Dale Carnegie and other self-help literature, it never seemed to translate into Jessica's behavior toward Bluma. The hopelessness and contempt filled up her lungs, and she dismissed the moment as "yeah, right, whatever." Never replied, never acknowledged it.

In 2017, our family reunited to celebrate Hanukkah. Intent on beginning a dialogue with Bluma, Jessica gathered up her courage and asked Bluma to take a walk with her. As we walked together, Jessica haltingly told Bluma about her realization. Bluma listened. Then, carefully, she answered, "You have a distorted way of remembering things."

Bluma felt a twinge of both compassion and pity for Jessica. She was not as scary as she used to be. She couldn't move well anymore, with calcified joints where she used to twist and turn, and punch and chase. But now, Bluma also felt indignant. She remembered the utter terror she'd felt around Jessica, the fear that her older, fearless sister would lash out and hit, punch or scratch her. That was abuse. She didn't think she was culpable for defending herself. How could the victim be blamed? And also, perhaps more importantly, Bluma thought, we'd both been subjected to a more imposing figure's abuse: our dad's. Though our parents had divorced some years earlier, the memory of our father's slaps, chases, insults and terror tactics were imprinted on Bluma's mind.

We couldn't see eye to eye, so the conversation ended, each of us disappointed and confused by the other's inability to see our reality. We retreated to our separate spheres and, once again, largely fell out of each other's lives. But that talk planted a seed.

Two years later, in October 2019, Bluma was living in Israel with her expanded family - a fifth baby had joined the gaggle - when an altercation in her community set her on her own path towards an epiphany. Bluma was part of a Community Center text-messaging group of English-speaking immigrants (designed to help alert them to programs being offered). A misguided suggestion by the city was made that special-needs children wear brightly colored bracelets to better alert parents and teachers to their different learning abilities.

The proposition was not malicious or ill-intended, just gauche. And it was clear immediately that it was a no-go.

But one mother who was especially outraged took the story to the press. Bluma felt the woman was lashing out and had overreacted when they'd already nixed the idea. Bluma sent her a text to express her concern. The woman's response was as sharp as a knife. She shot Bluma down, telling her she was an author and answered to no one. Bluma sensed an old rage rise up in her. She couldn't stand the woman's sense of entitlement, impulsiveness and ferocity. It was a dead ringer for Jessica. So Bluma went on the offensive. In a flash, she knew exactly what she could say to this woman to crush her: she knew just which insecurities to zero in on and which buttons to push to make her feel unhinged. It was uncanny, and frightening, like a Marvel character's instantaneous transformation into a superhero, or villain. As the words arranged themselves in Bluma's head, ready to fire, she realized that if she went ahead, she would no longer be the victim in this situation. She would be the bully.

Bluma dropped the conversation with the woman and went for a walk in her neighborhood. As she wound her way around the stone paths, she thought about Jessica. She pulled her phone out and started recording herself thinking aloud. Growing up, she realized she'd deployed this super-power on her older sister, weaponizing her words in a way she knew would hurt her. Because Jessica routinely beat her up, Bluma had always considered herself a victim. But now she could see that the way she attacked Jessica verbally - which she'd always considered a defense mechanism - was also abuse. She now understood what Jessica had tried to say to her two years prior. They had abused each other growing up. Bluma recorded a five-minute message. When she was done, she sent the audio to her sister.

Just as Jessica's commitment to self improvement had helped her reflect on her childhood and reach her epiphany about our relationship, Bluma's work as a psychologist, mainly working with couples (dyads/pairs), had given her a deeper understanding of conflicts in relationships. The division between who was right and who was wrong was rarely clear-cut between the couples she counseled. It took two to tango. Now she thought to herself, the same is true for siblings.

A little more than 7,000 miles across the globe, Jessica was on a real estate call, across the street from where she lived, when she got the message. She braced herself for a verbal attack - that was all she knew from Bluma - and quickly and cautiously listened. She could hardly believe what she was hearing - she even told her client about it. She finished her call, then sent an audio back. She reiterated that we had grown up in chaos, and that she was proud of having emerged from it to become a decent person, a hard worker and a good mother.

Back in Israel, as Bluma cleaned up after dinner, she gingerly listened to Jessica's response. But at her mention of being a good mother, a familiar feeling of anger and outrage rose up in her throat. When Jessica called herself a good mother, to Bluma it sounded like Jessica was again acting with superiority, assuming Bluma needed to be schooled. It felt like a provocation. So once again that day, Bluma felt the words align themselves in her mind, ready for take down. She fired back with an audio, putting Jessica back in her place. Then Bluma went upstairs and jumped in the shower.

As the water trickled down, sadness and shame washed over her. "What have you done? Why did you do it?" she thought to herself. "Of course Jessica is a good mother, you should give her that." She had not wanted to send Jessica an angry audio; her heart and soul screamed, "Don't do it, Bluma!" But something beyond her control had compelled her to do it anyway. She felt powerless. Then, in a flash of clarity, she heard God say, "She is where you need to go," Breathless, she dashed out of the shower, wrapped a towel around herself and grabbed her phone. She called Jessica, who picked up. "I need to see your face," Bluma said urgently. Jessica agreed to FaceTime.

"Jess, I did it again," Bluma said. "I can't live like this. I can't be controlled by this dynamic between us," Bluma told her. "Me neither," Jessica responded. Bluma shared the message she'd heard from God. And we understood. The divine message Bluma heard, "*she* is where *you* need to go" was both of us. It was Bluma. It was Jessica. It was all siblings in the world. Your sibling is where you need to go. It isn't your side or their side, it is both sides. Both have value, both are important, but most importantly, both are necessary to allow a new path to emerge, releasing you both from the hold your pain held.

And for the first time in our lives, at 46 and 49 years old, we talked. We really talked about how this toxic dynamic between us continued to control our lives despite our best efforts to turn away from it and pretend it didn't matter. We simply could not escape it on our own, individually. So that day, we decided to face it together.

Over the next year, we'd end up doing just that, and it would change our lives forever for the better.

We know our childhood story is far from unique. For many, sibling relationships are the longest-lasting ties you will ever have with anyone in your life. Just think about it this way: you may know your parents between 30 and 60 years - hopefully more - but you're likely to have your siblings for upwards of 80 years. These are the people with whom you share your genetics, your family history, and the fundamental experiences that make up who you are today. And yet, so many of us let these foundational relationships wither, sour, or simply fade away.

As adults building separate lives in separate homes and cities, we tried to move past the antagonism that had defined so much of our youth. Individually, we did the work. We each went to therapy. When we became parents, we each separately took stock of what we thought our parents had done right, and what they'd done wrong, and we course-corrected. But any inner peace we'd reach on our own would be shattered the moment we crossed paths. We simply could not stop triggering each other. And the sense of frustration and inadequacy we aroused in each other permeated every aspect of our lives. The traumatic and tumultuous relationship that we had as sisters affected our friendships, romantic relationships and even our careers. Even though we didn't realize it, we were controlled by our toxic dynamic.

According to Psychology Today, up to *80% of kids experience some form of sibling cruelty*. So, we know you can relate. And we have great news. You're already on your way towards transforming your dynamic. The simple fact that you are taking the time to read these words means that you are curious about how to change your sibling relationship, and that's a powerful start. You have a choice. You don't have to let the dynamic control you anymore. You can take back the reins, or "take a different turn,"[2] as a friend once told us, and change directions. You can set yourself free. We will guide you through your journey.

On that day in November 2019, we decided to "take a different turn", and it transformed our lives. We saw that, in order to heal from the past we had to move *through* it as a team, by revisiting the past we created with each other. We saw that what was integral to our healing was having a balance between each of our experiences, in order to witness it from each perspective. We knew we had to work together, but there was no roadmap to do this. So we created **SibHub**[3]: the place for everything Sibling-related. This book is our guide to GROWING UP YOUR SIBLING RELATIONSHIP.

Over the course of thousands of hours of Zoom calls spanning three years, we reflected on our childhood to understand how our experiences and the roles we were given in our family had shaped the adults we had become, and how they had driven our actions ever since. But the change was swift. Within four weeks, we felt a growing peace within our relationship. By basing our new exchanges in compassion, curiosity, forgiveness and understanding - some of the qualities we call our Prime Directive, and which we'll share with you in this book - we very quickly transformed our dynamic from

---

2 "Roots Tour" documentary.

3 www.yoursibhub.com

one saddled by competition to one defined by cooperation. For the first time, we felt like we were on the same team, working to accomplish the same mission. And ultimately, we managed to bridge the gap that had alienated us from each other for so many years.

Today, our relationship no longer feels like a burden, but a bond that has set us free. We are happy to call ourselves sisters, friends and partners. Once we began healing our relationship and ourselves, we found that so many other areas of our lives underwent a profound transformation as well. We have discovered a path forward. We now know what it takes to reset adult sibling relationships. And we want this gift for you too. In addition to excavating our own memories, we dug into insights derived from both hard sciences, like physics and biology, and soft sciences, like psychology and sociology, in order to create a framework that was fine-tuned, fast and structured. In only a matter of weeks, you will be on your way towards life-changing transformations, just like what we experienced. Let us guide you to the other side and together help you and your sibling reframe the past to a beautiful new future.

Since you are reading this, you are seeking to know how to move beyond past pain and create a new dynamic with your sibling. It wasn't long ago that we were in your shoes: full of questions and concerns. We know you may feel scared and worried that you'll be putting in a lot of time and effort for nothing, or for more disappointment. Since we started this process, we've talked to many siblings who've told us, "Good for you, but there's no way I could do that." In fact, that's what Jessica's real estate client told her that day in 2019 when we finally agreed to work on our relationship together. Jessica was so shocked by Bluma's voice mail telling her she agreed with her - that we'd been abusive to each other growing up - that she couldn't help but tell the client about it. The client told Jessica to keep her hopes down: she, herself, came from a complicated family in which she'd always felt like the Black Sheep. She'd tried to reconnect with her siblings for years, and it hadn't worked. It was a lost cause.

We know that so many people feel that way. But we repaired our relationship. We did it, and we truly know you can, too. Plus, you're not doing it alone. We're right here with you. We'll be guiding you every step of the way. This book is for every person out there who feels like Jessica's real estate client did: that their sibling relationship is hopeless. It's not. And we'll work on it together. We've got you.

Based on our experience, and our evidence-based research, we've created a first-of-it's-kind process for adult sibling healing. We are confident it will take you where you want to go.

In the following chapters, we'll explain why sibling relationships can cause so much conflict. We'll talk about how the role you were assigned in your family contributed to this difficult dynamic. We'll also explore how your relationship with your parents - and the relationship they had with theirs - affected **your** sibling dynamic. We'll touch on psychology, neurology, quantum physics and biology. Then we'll show you exactly which steps to take in order to heal yourself and your sibling relationship. We want you to know it's possible to process your past pain and move forward united. It's possible to live a fuller, healthier life and to repair a broken relationship you never imagined could be fixed. You can heal. You can soar.

Trust us—it's worth it.

Chapter recap:

- After surviving a chaotic childhood in our dysfunctional family, we thought we'd be better off without each other. But the toxic relationship that we developed as sisters affected every aspect of our lives, from our friendships and romantic relationships to our careers.

- *We realized that in order to move beyond our difficult past, we had to process it together, as a team.*

- *We developed a process to heal adult sibling relationships and we're here to help you heal, too.*

CHAPTER 2

Why You Need To Heal Your Sibling Relationship

Healing your sibling relationship will profoundly change your life. It's a difficult point to make in a culture that often downplays sibling violence as a normal part of human development. Scenes of children running around a yard or kitchen table trying to "kill" each other are a hallmark of our favorite movies and television shows. In real life, we call that "roughhousing" or "boys will be boys" (though we know girls can throw punches, too). And of course, some degree of friction is completely normal and even healthy: we don't come out of the womb knowing how to resolve conflict like tiny suit-wearing diplomats.

But there is an enormous difference between siblings occasionally jostling each other in an otherwise loving and supportive relationship, and siblings actively and consistently making each other's lives miserable. That's the difference between sibling rivalry and sibling abuse.

Let's break this down. Sibling rivalry is situational. Imagine two young brothers. Let's call them Alex and Theo. Alex, who's 4, and Theo, who's 8, are either thick as thieves, or driving each other nuts. They live in an apartment building with their parents and other siblings, and every morning on their way out to school, Alex (4) rushes out to get to the elevator first to press the button. It's his thing. Theo (8) knows this, and every once in a while, just to annoy Alex, he races out of the apartment to push the button before his brother. To Theo, this is hilarious. To Alex, it's infuriating. To everyone else, it's annoying. The point is, it's behavior that creates friction between the brothers, but it's pretty forgettable in the grand scheme of things. They get along most of the time. It is in this particular situation - the elevator before school - that there is conflict.

Sibling abuse, on the other hand, is intentional. If Alex and Theo constantly behaved like this - if at every occasion, Theo found an opportunity to take something away from Alex and make him feel bad, and Alex always responded by fighting back - then their friction would no longer be caused by specific circumstances. It would be the nature of their relationship. There would be no good-enough moments to offset the barrage of actions meant to undermine and hurt each other. Their behavior would be an internal choice to turn each other into punching bags and offload all their pain and frustration onto each other.

Sibling rivalry is a set of punctuated moments that are part of a fabric of love, warmth and goodness. It's typical. It's minimal. It's not incessant, and it doesn't define the relationship.

Sibling abuse is chronic and unyielding. You're always on the lookout for the next attack, but somehow you still feel blindsided and unprepared when it comes. Part of our mission with this book is to make sure people stop considering sibling abuse as rivalry. That's a harmful and dangerous confusion.

According to a <u>1980 study</u> by Straus, Gelles and Steinmetz, sibling abuse occurred in more than 60 percent of families in the US, *making sibling violence the most common form of domestic violence.* That means that 6 out of 10 families have experienced sibling abuse. No comprehensive study on sibling abuse has been conducted since then. By contrast, intimate partner violence has, in the last few decades, garnered increased awareness and attention. We now know that <u>41% of women and 26% of men</u> in the US have experienced sexual violence, physical violence, and/or stalking by an intimate partner, according to the Center for Disease Control and Prevention. The awareness and attention of the scope of intimate partner abuse led to the enactment of anti-domestic violence campaigns and resources for victims. The same has not happened with sibling abuse. The lack of awareness of sibling abuse, and consequently, the lack of help, has devastating consequences for all of us. As we'll show in this book, learning how to manage conflict with your sibling allows you to handle conflict with other people in your life. Putting an end to sibling violence could be the first step to ending the broader cycle of violence.

Sibling abuse is basically like living with a schoolyard bully, except you have no home to seek safe refuge. While there's public awareness that we should intervene or call the police when we suspect a child is being mistreated by their parents, we are not encouraged to step in when we see siblings mistreating each other. In this sense, our society is complicit in allowing sibling violence. Bluma will always remember the time when, as an adult, she visited the rabbi who lived down the street from our childhood home and, unprompted, he told her, "I never thought anything normal would come out of your household." He'd seen, firsthand, the chaos and dysfunction of our family, and he had done nothing. Perhaps he thought someone else would step in. He might have felt hesitant to "poke the bear" and receive our dad's wrath. Whatever his motive was, he stayed on the sidelines.

This kind of inaction - when we avoid helping someone, expecting others to intervene - is called bystander apathy and serves two purposes. First, it excuses us from our responsibility to act, leaving us free from the burden we might have felt to do something. Second, it saves us from the potential regret of intervening and failing to actually help. Basically, bystander apathy is like a little voice in your head telling you it's for the best if you avoid the messiness of getting involved in something that does not directly affect you. It's incredibly common. Of course, everyone is different; some people are more likely to get involved than others, and from one culture to the next, intervening in other people's problems might be more or less acceptable. **The point here is, bystander apathy is problematic when it comes to sibling abuse: it allows for and reinforces toxic dynamics to persist, unmonitored, in perpetuity.**

In our case, our sibling rivalry very quickly turned into sibling abuse, and we both carried visible and invisible marks of each other's abuse on our bodies and in our psyches until we set our pain free by doing this work together. There is often a power differential in abusive relationships, in which one party is dominant, and the other is submissive. While those roles can be fixed in certain abusive sibling relationships, in many, like ours, they seesaw. One day Jessica could be the aggressor and Bluma the victim, and the next day we would switch - Bluma would be the aggressor and Jessica the victim. The point is that our attacks were constant and sowed fear and doubt in our minds and hearts. We never knew when the next onslaught would come, but we knew it was always right around the corner. We lived on the lookout, especially around each other.

This is a heavy weight to carry around, and it becomes exponentially more burdensome as the years pass by. It shapes who you are, lingers inside you and follows you. It leaves you suspended in a constant state of fight, flight or freeze (we'll explore this in Chapter 3). It warps your view of the world by forcing you to see everything through the lens of your sibling paradigm. And most of the time you don't even know it. It controls you in ways of which you're not consciously aware.

We started to realize this when we became mothers ourselves and struggled not to project our understanding of each other onto our children. It was a knee-jerk reaction: when Jessica's daughter would start wailing in her car seat for no apparent reason, Jessica would see Bluma in her. When Bluma's son would react to his sister's attack by hitting her five times harder, Bluma would see Jessica in him. As individuals, we each had to consciously try not to transfer our burdens onto our kids, and instead see them for who they were - NOT as stand-ins for each other.

The crazy thing is that most people who've suffered from sibling abuse aren't ever aware of its far-reaching effects and consequences, because as a society, we don't talk about it. What's worse is that we accept it as normal. We want sibling relationships to be valued and be a topic discussed in society.

Just like most people, we didn't realize our broken bond was impacting every other aspect of our lives, way beyond how we raised our children - from our education and careers to our romantic relationships and friendships. But really, it makes sense.

Siblings have an extraordinary amount of influence over us. From infancy through childhood and adolescence and all the way to adulthood, everything we watch and learn from our siblings impacts our emotional and social development. Our siblings are our first friends and primal rivals. For better or for worse, they are our first role models. From them, we learn how to talk to another child on the playground, how to respond to a teacher at school, and how to build and keep friendships. They teach us how to trust or protect ourselves in a world with other people. Ultimately, our sibling relationships undergird how we learn to operate socially in the world.

Most relationships are not black and white, much as we might like them to be. How much easier would it be for things to be clearly one way or another? Yet, they're usually gradients of gray. In the context of sibling relationships, very rarely are they either completely rooted in rivalry, or completely devoid of it. They involve a mix of rivalry and its opposite, revelry. It's so important to understand that your relationship is somewhere on this continuum, meaning that there is room for improvement, but also, that it's not all bad - that at heart, there is also love. A nuanced understanding of your sibling relationship, in which you see both the good <u>and</u> the bad, will help you better understand how your relationship has impacted the ways you socialize with others.

Human beings are complex creatures. We can feel one emotion intensely or feel multiple at the same time. As we develop into adults, the black-and-white, single-focused thinking of our childhood, <u>"Mad", "Sad", "Bad", "Glad"</u> (page 32-35), gives way to more abstract gray areas like a Likert scale of variations, so we can effectively weather a range of experiences. This helps us cope with the complexity of adulthood and react appropriately to events. For example, we might sigh when something mildly disappointing happens, or allow ourselves to cry if something drastically disappointing takes place. But most of us don't cry for the mildly disappointing event. We have a range.

Mad, Sad, Bad, Glad Exercise

Mad
NAME IT TO CLAIM IT!

LOW INTENSITY
- Annoyed
- Displeased
- Upset
- Discontent
- Irked
- Frustrated (can fit here too, depending on context)
- Skeptical
- Sarcastic

MEDIUM INTENSITY
- Angry
- Resentful
- Jealous
- Insecure
- Hurt
- Threatened
- Critical
- Distant

HIGH INTENSITY
- Furious
- Enraged
- Hostile
- Provoked
- Violated
- Devastated
- Vengeful

Sad
NAME IT TO CLAIM IT!

HIGH INTENSITY
- Depressed
- Despair
- Isolated
- Powerless
- Empty
- Loathing
- Revulsion
- Detestable

MEDIUM INTENSITY
- Lonely
- Abandoned
- Remorseful
- Ashamed
- Vulnerable
- Ignored
- Disapproval

LOW INTENSITY
- Disappointed
- Bored
- Indifferent/Numb
- Hesitant
- Guilt
- Awful (can fit here depending on context)
- Avoidance
- Judgmental

Mad, Sad, Bad, Glad Exercise

Bad
NAME IT TO CLAIM IT!

LOW INTENSITY
- Confused
- Worried
- Scared
- Startled
- Insecure
- Overwhelmed
- Perplexed
- Ridiculed

MEDIUM INTENSITY
- Disrespected
- Alienated
- Inadequate
- Insignificant
- Frightened
- Dismayed
- Terrified

HIGH INTENSITY
- Humiliated
- Rejected
- Worthless
- Inferior
- Shocked
- Disillusioned
- Astonished
- Submissive
- Invisible

Glad

NAME IT TO CLAIM IT!

LOW INTENSITY
- Interested
- Amused
- Eager
- Open
- Playful
- Optimistic
- Energetic
- Happy
- Discontent

MEDIUM INTENSITY
- Hopeful
- Proud
- Accepted
- Confident
- Important
- Powerful
- Loving
- Fulfilled
- Belonging
- Elated

HIGH INTENSITY
- Ecstatic
- Liberated
- Inspired
- Joyful
- Peaceful
- Courageous
- Intimate
- Provocative
- Empowered
- Attached / Connected
- Splendid

When you feel rooted in a pain from your past, this is harder to do. You often feel trapped in a binary experience that leaves you with limited options. Events and people are good or bad. Black or white. Right or wrong. Mad or glad.

Once you expand your perspectives on each other, you begin to have more space for the layers, the degrees, the multiplicity of who each of you are, and who you can become. That's what happened for us. Now, instead of thinking in terms of black and white, we think in shades of gray, offering an expanded view of reality. So, instead of binary options, you get a continuum (see chart on page 32-35).

Tom Robbins once said, "There are two kinds of people in this world: Those who believe there are two kinds of people in this world, and those who are smart enough to know better." We couldn't agree more.

We invite you to use our continuums to identify the ranges of experiences you have had with siblings, parents and socially. We found that it helped us to stay open when we recognize that we are more than just the label from our past - that our scope of experiences has given us access to a breadth AND depth now, and that looking honestly and authentically at our past, through the present lens, allows us to create an unmapped, unburdened future.

Take a look at the Sibling Continuum on page 38 and think about where on it your relationship sits today. To help you understand the range, we've listed words which are common in sibling relationships, and that are generally 2 sides of the same coin, which may be experienced as mild, medium or spicy, depending on the situation. What role do feelings and qualities like competition and sabotage have? How rivalrous were you then versus now? How much cooperation and support existed in your sibling relationship then versus now? How revelrous would you like to become? There is a multiplicity of ways you can feel toward your sibling, both then and now.

Sibling Continuum

Rivalry

- Competition | Cooperation
- Sabotage | Support
- Restrictive | Unlimited
- Argumentative | Collaborative
- Withholding | Validating
- Excluding | Including
- Depreciate | Appreciate
- Regress | Evolve
- Leaning Away | Leaning In
- Perish | Flourish
- Enemies | Allies

Revelry

As you see from the Sibling Continuum, there are many ways siblings can show up. Now that you have had a chance to think about what kinds of feelings your own sibling relationship brings up, think about how often you experience these same feelings in your other relationships. Do you see a pattern?

Write out what patterns you see:

_____

_____

_____

_____

_____

Once we started thinking about where we fell on the sibling continuum, we were able to see how much our dynamic affected our relationships with other people in our lives. The ways we coped with the conflict and tension between us became our rule of thumb for how to deal with others. Because we were always expecting a fight between us, we also unconsciously were always on the lookout for conflict with others, too.

We want to share an example with you from both of our lives to illustrate this. Tellingly, both of these events took place after we'd left home, at times when we were both trying to become the adults we wanted to be, away from the chaos of our family nest. But as you'll see, something was standing in the way of that.

We'll start with Bluma.

Growing up, I was never concerned about getting good grades in school. I just wanted to socialize and have fun. Luckily, I still managed to get decent grades by cracking a book open at the last minute and relying on my memory and clever wits to make the grade. I never wanted to be valedictorian, but my teachers had to grudgingly admit I was doing just fine. That all changed in graduate school, when I finally embarked on my journey to become a psychologist. Suddenly, nothing seemed more important than my studies, and the material was not easy. I worked my butt off, balancing classes, papers, group projects, exams, oral presentations, two internships and a job. Overall, I was doing pretty well - except in this one class. From day one, I could tell my Theories of Personality professor did not like me. He was hard on me in a way that elicited my classmates' sympathy: one day, during a break, a few asked me if I needed a hug after he'd been particularly hard on me. And this didn't last a semester only - he had taught me for three years. It was three years of hell. I was almost at my breaking point, seriously considering dropping out of the class, when I finally decided to confront him. "What is your problem with me?" I asked him. And he told me, "You ask me questions like you think I don't understand."

Bluma's professor had mentioned in class that he was the younger twin and alluded to feeling in competition with his twin brother, saying he felt his twin had pushed him out of the way so that he could exit the womb first. It made sense that living a lifetime with this belief left him vulnerable to feelings of inferiority, wanting instead to have superiority whenever possible. Being in a position of authority as the professor, gave him just that - until he met Bluma, with her equally present superiority-inferiority complex. By speaking her mind in class - occasionally disagreeing or contradicting her professor - Bluma was triggering this complex. Her professor's hostility was a dead ringer for the negative energy she remembered feeling around Jessica. It triggered the same disproportionate anger. That's why she couldn't let it roll off her back. From a young age, Bluma had been primed to fight back with her words whenever she felt like someone was challenging her. But, here, this was working against her with her professor–she was allowing her sibling relic to drive her interactions, feeling unsafe rather than empowered.

Basically, Bluma and her professor were a perfect storm of mismatched sibling complexes. But she didn't realize it at the time. Now, looking back, Bluma can see that if she'd only approached her professor earlier, or understood the source of their adversarial relationship, she could have saved herself three years of pain.

Now let's show you Jessica's example. You'll see that it has many similar notes.

Unlike Bluma, Jessica had always struggled in school. Despite being curious and working harder than almost anyone in her class, Jessica's ability to pass a test was like playing Russian Roulette. Her dyslexia simply made it impossible to know whether all her efforts would actually pay off. After graduating high school, she enrolled in a women's college and, in her first year, took a class on broadcasting . This, at last, was in her wheelhouse. She knew radio stations like the back of her hand, since her parents had owned a few. Growing up around broadcasting, she knew the jargon and the tools, and didn't hesitate to shoot her hand in the air to share her knowledge, often contradicting her professor when the professor got it wrong. The result was that they often clashed. To Jessica, it was clear her real-world experience gave her an expertise her textbook-abiding professor simply did not have. But her professor bristled at the interruptions. And the one class Jessica looked forward to became a source of frustration.

In retrospect, Jessica understands that her desire to set the record straight, even if it meant undermining her professor's authority, was partially borne of a need to prove her intelligence, and be celebrated for it. Her professor, by insisting that she knew more than Jessica, became a stand-in for Bluma, who, for so much of their childhood, had challenged her knowledge and diminished her intelligence. So Jessica felt the need to keep on asserting herself in the classroom.

But like Bluma and her professor, all of this precious information was not available to Jessica back then. Today, understanding this, she thinks she could have gotten curious to learn something new, or offered up her radio information in a way that caused less friction, or said nothing at all.

These are two examples that show how our sibling dynamic, and the way we learned to deal with conflict, seeped into our adult relationships and careers. We were both unknowingly tethered to our sibling dynamic, and any future relationship that reminded us of it yanked us back into the same trap. We'd feel this disproportionate reaction - this feeling of anger, this desire to be heard - to both the person in front of us, but also to each other, since these people, like our professors, were stand-ins, sibling doppelgängers for Jessica and Bluma. We simply couldn't disengage from this negative energy-pattern.

You've probably experienced this too. Think back: have you ever met someone who immediately triggered you, just like your sibling did? Who made you feel inferior, sad, or mad just like your brother or sister would? Often, this happens subconsciously - you may not even realize you're making the connection. You become dysregulated - activated by sensory similarities and familiar fears. Your reaction becomes an emotional outburst to strangers and loved ones alike. And now that we are pointing this experience out, you will start becoming more aware of these sibling 'twins' showing up at work, at home or in your friendship dynamics.

We only started understanding this after we decided to work on our relationship and delve into our past shared pains. That, in turn, allowed us to revisit some of the more painful or dramatic chapters of our lives to understand exactly why we acted and reacted the way we did. Once we healed the roots of our original sibling stories, we released the burdens we'd carried against each other - and the demand to defend them. And moments like the interactions with our professors just didn't cut as deep anymore.

There's nothing more empowering than understanding yourself and your drives. By integrating past healed pains, you free up all the space inside you that used to be taken up by loud, unresolved conflicts from your childhood. Suddenly, you have the bandwidth to learn how to holistically deal with conflict. You are aware of your responses and feel less reactive. It's more of a whisper now.

Because here's the truth: unprocessed past trauma keeps you stuck in the past.

Think of it this way. Remember a time when, while talking to a friend, you were trying to recall the name of a song the two of you used to love, and it simply wouldn't come to you? It was on the tip of your tongue but simply kept escaping you. Then, days later, it finally popped into your head when you weren't actively thinking about it, while you were driving home. Bingo! It was Journey's "Don't Stop Believin'." Then you shrugged it off and kept on driving. What happened was a phenomenon called the Zeigarnik Effect, after the Soviet psychologist Bluma Zeigarnik who recognized it. It explains how our brains can hold tons of critical information for short periods of time while we work out solutions to immediate problems or issues. Once we've solved those problems, our brains let go of the information. Basically, on an unconscious level, your brain was *working the whole time between the conversation* with your friend and your drive home to remember the name of that song. Your brain was stuck on a problem-solving loop until it found the answer, at which point it was finally free to move on.

When you've had a negative or traumatic event in your life and have not processed it, your brain gets stuck on that problem-solving loop as well. This also applies to sibling relationships. When a sibling pair has conflict in the past and has never resolved it, each person holds onto some aspect of how they were wronged. Your brains continue to work cyclically to try to resolve the issue. That's why a fight from your childhood can continue to preoccupy you for years and years. It's because you are trying to resolve, understand and close the loop on a confusing set of circumstances you never fully worked through. As soon as you do, the weight that you've carried, the pain and confusion that has driven and dominated you, finally evaporates, freeing you from the past's shackles.

So if you've been looping on this "one continuous fight" from your childhood, you're not alone. Your brain simply hasn't had the chance to finish solving the problem. There's nothing wrong with you.

That's what was happening to us. It was only by healing our relationship that we finally closed the loop and moved on, with more generosity, grace and respect for each other, and for others. And that's what fixing your sibling relationship will allow you to do.

The beauty of the process we're sharing with you is that it proves there's always time to close the loop, heal your relationship, and learn healthy conflict resolution skills that are truly the bedrock of any functioning relationship, whether that be a friendship, romantic partner, or business associate. To unlock this ability to fruitfully engage with the world around you, we wholeheartedly believe you must start by (re)learning these skills with your sibling.

Dan Siegel, the founding director of the Mindful Awareness Research Center at UCLA, conducted groundbreaking research on the neurobiology of collectives. He found that we're not wired to function individually, but rather as part of a group. Basically, you're not wired to be a "me," you're wired to be a "we." And that's why conflict resolution - which usually implicates two or more sides - requires all parties involved to participate. This is the logic behind couple's therapy. If you could solve your marriage problems alone, you would. But you can't. It takes two people interacting and working in unison to do it. No amount of soul-searching will help save your marriage if you both aren't there to witness it, understand each other's pain, and agree to build a better connection together. The same goes for broken sibling relationships.

The harm we both suffered from one another was so clear to us that we each searched for ways to heal, individually. We both did soul-searching and went to therapy. But as hard as we worked on ourselves individually, we simply couldn't heal *entirely*. We were like rowers in two separate boats, each pushing our oars on a single side, going round and round in circles. We simply needed to hop into one boat and start rowing together, coordinating our movements to the same rhythm, and finally move forward. That's what we did when we finally decided to do the work together.

(A quick note: we're operating off Dan Siegel's logic in this book, which is why we've written it for siblings, in the plural. And we recognize the fact that some people won't have the chance to do this work with their sibling due to a death, or perhaps even because you're an only child. We understand that. You can still find peace on your own. We'll address this in a future publication.)

Chapter recap:

- Society downplays sibling violence as a normal, "boys will be boys" phase of development. But that means we often confuse healthy sibling rivalry with toxic sibling abuse, which are two very different things.

- Studies show that sibling abuse is one of the most common forms of domestic violence.

- Because your siblings are your first friends and rivals, your relationships with them become your models for engaging with and reacting to other people. If you don't handle conflict well with your siblings, you struggle to handle conflict well with everyone else.

- Just like in couple's counseling, you can't fix a broken relationship on your own. You need to do it as a team. In order to learn healthy conflict resolution skills, you have to do the work with your sibling.

CHAPTER 3

How Your Parents Affect Your Sibling Relationship

We've talked about how your sibling relationship plays a crucial role in shaping the way you interact with other people and engage with the world around you. Now it's time to step back in time to look at how your sibling relationship is formed in the first place. Because your sibling dynamic doesn't just create itself. It doesn't exist in a vacuum. It's molded by a powerful force outside both you and your sibling's control: the all-encompassing force of your parents.

We are all unique human beings with unique personalities and experiences, so the ways we relate to each other are bound to be different. That's certainly the case between you and your parents. You will have a distinct relationship with each of your parents, and your sibling will have their own unique relationship with them, too. In turn, these different dynamics between parents and children proliferate and have profound effects on sibling relationships.

Growing up, you have a front-row seat to the theater that is your family: you can see exactly how your parents speak to and behave differently with each family member. For example, say Jake's dad asks his slightly older brother to throw a baseball around most Sunday afternoons, but not him. Or his mom is more lenient with his younger sister when she gets up to no good in a way that she isn't with Jake. They'll both notice these different attitudes, and that will change how each sibling sees the other, and how they interact, too.

On top of that, parents act as barometers *signaling* what kids can and can't get away with in their behaviors with each other. Say in a family of four kids, Max, the second youngest, gets picked on by his other siblings. When Max's siblings call him names or hide his lunch box, his dad doesn't say anything. If they twist Max's arm, however, then their dad intervenes and yells at them. What's happening here is that Max's siblings are comparing behaviors with responses and are learning just how far they can push the envelope. They learn that they won't get in trouble if they tease or play tricks on their brother, but they know that if they hurt him physically, they risk receiving negative consequences. That's the line they shouldn't cross. What's being created is a cost-benefit, risk-reward, stimulus-response paradigm that sets the rhythm for how siblings will treat each other. And that paradigm is being built from children's perception of how much each one of them is valued by each parent.

In the last chapter, we shared the sibling continuum with you. The nature of your relationships with your parents is another continuum that significantly affects how you go on to engage with other people in your life. This one does not hinge on the place between revelry and rivalry, but rather, between acceptance and rejection. We base the following continuum off the work of psychologist Ronald Rohner, the author of the interpersonal acceptance-rejection theory (IPARTheory), which says that across cultures and demographics, people's psychological and behavioral adjustment depends on how accepted or rejected they felt by their parents in their early years. This is a universal principle: Rohner conducted his research in 28 countries, from the US to China to Bahrain, and across social classes and ethnicities. And the key here is **perception**. Rohner found that people's beliefs about how much their parents accepted or rejected them - and not necessarily how accurate their perceptions were - are what affected their development.

Just like sibling relationships are typically not 100% marked by either rivalry or revelry, our relationships with our parents - or how we perceive them - are not completely characterized by either rejection or acceptance. We'd like you to take a look at the following Parental Continuum (page 53). Remember what we shared in Chapter 2: we found that Continuums helped us to stay open when we recognized that we are more than just the label from our past, that our scope of experiences has given us access to a breadth AND depth now, and that looking honestly and authentically at our past through the present lens allows us to create an unmapped, unburdened future. So, consider the list of qualities and feelings that align with the two ends of the continuum. Where do you think you land on these different feeling experiences? What was in conflict, what wasn't? Create a picture of the ways you had, have and want to have a relationship with each of your parents, using the ranges of experiences to light the way.

Parental Continuum

Acceptance

EMOTIONAL
Unreliable | Dependable
Unsympathetic | Sympathetic
Disapproving | Encouraging
Indifferent | Interested
Scolding | Praising
Insulting | Complimentary
Offensive | Soothing
Ridiculing | Accepting
Distant | Engaging
Cold | Warm
Withdraws love | Nurtures love
Negative Comparisons | Acceptance of Personality
View as a burden | View as a pleasure

PHYSICAL
Hitting | Hugging/Kissing
Grabbing | Caressing
Hostility | Comforting
Unaffectionate/Aggressive | Affectionate (cuddling)
Physically Absent (unavailable) | Physically Present (attentive)

Rejection

How relevant are feelings and qualities like unreliable or distant? Praising and warm? Do you feel like your parents, or one of them, is absent or unavailable? Or do you feel their affection? Just like with the sibling continuum, you probably will have connected with words from both columns. Now think about whether some of these same feelings come up when you think about your relationships with other people in your life. Do you notice a pattern?

In our family, our relationships with our parents heavily impacted how we felt about each other and informed the ways we treated - and mistreated - each other. In the following paragraphs, we'll paint a picture of our relationships with our mom and dad to elicit the dynamics at play in our family unit, and show how these contributed to our hostility. As you read along, we invite you to think about your own family and look at the individual relationships you have with each member.

Bluma's earliest memory of our mom is one of pure delight. She's sitting in her lap facing her, her legs dangling at her side, the two of them laughing. She feels safe and loved. From the get-go, the two of them simply clicked. There was the fact that at barely two, Bluma was rushed to the hospital after accidentally overdosing on narcotics. The near loss of such a young child may have made Bluma all the more precious to our mom. On top of that, Bluma started speaking so early, it was easy for the two of them to communicate. Bluma loved being near our mom and followed her around the house, enjoying watching her do mundane tasks like household chores or makeup. They connected on a deep level, and this connection only matured with age. Bluma was the only one in our family to accompany our mom to Temple nearly every Friday night - not necessarily because she loved going, but so that our mom wouldn't be alone. She wrote our mom frequent letters and notes to apologize for a fight or show her love and appreciation. After our parents divorced, she acted as a confidant when our mom started dating again. To this day, Bluma and our mom consider each other best friends.

This loving and supportive relationship was so important to Bluma growing up, partly because it was a counter to the difficult relationship she had with our dad. Bluma was often scared of him. In fourth grade, after procrastinating on a school project and only getting started on it at 9 PM the night before it was due, he went into a rage, hurling her books and papers off the table, shouting while Bluma cowered behind a chair. No apology. No repair. When she skipped a sleepover and instead went out to meet up with her boyfriend at a party in 7th grade, our dad tracked her down and dragged her out, pulling her shirt so hard it ripped. On the drive home, enraged, he slammed on the brakes, twisted back from the driver's seat and grabbed her collar, pulling her downward and started punching her on her back, calling her a slut and a whore. Bluma remembers feeling so humiliated, scared and hurt. These are just two examples among many in which Bluma remembers feeling terrified and powerless before our dad's rage. She once ran away from home for three days because she was so tired of this never-ending cycle of our dad blowing up, offering no apology or repair, and expecting everyone to simply carry on.

Meanwhile, Jessica has a different understanding of the man. She also had to deal with our dad's eruptions, but if he hit her, she'd hit him right back. She was also scared of him, like Bluma was, but she felt like she had to stand up to him. The time that he beat Bluma after dragging her out of that party, Jessica, a high schooler, put an end to it by yelling at our dad to stop and then by running away, forcing him to chase her, giving Bluma a reprieve. Our dad could be just as mean with Jessica as he was with Bluma, but he also had a soft spot for her. They both coped with dyslexia and had a similar resolve and temperament, which endeared her to him. He taught Jessica to believe in herself, and told her she was beautiful and just as capable as anyone else (as opposed to what he told Bluma). With Jessica, he occasionally apologized after flying into a rage. Their relationship was certainly complicated, but it wasn't pure torment the way it was for Bluma. Because for Jessica, our dad wasn't any worse than our mom.

Jessica and our mom have always been a mismatch of energy. Jessica was an active and headstrong child: she wanted to do everything and do it all herself with no help from anyone else. When she was still in diapers, our mom would have to cover the entire kitchen floor with newspaper at mealtimes in preparation for the splatter: Jessica had a great time flicking her food everywhere like a baby Jackson Pollock. Jessica was just bursting with energy, and our mom found it exhausting and a bit scary. Because of Jessica's dyslexia, our mom had to devote much of her parenting to making sure Jessica was still getting a good education. She helped Jessica with her homework after school. It was a painful and protracted process that could take up hours in the afternoon, and often ended with both of them yelling and crying. If our mom showered Bluma with affection, she held back with Jessica. She loved Jessica, certainly, and told her so with her words, but she didn't seem to particularly like her. And Jessica didn't *feel* loved.

These different connections created tensions and patterns between us in both direct and indirect ways. Our dad's approach to conflict - blowing up, then expecting everyone to move on - influenced the way we fought, without taking any time to resolve, and without knowing how to repair. Our mom's aversion to conflict, her closeness with Bluma and her feelings of confusion about Jessica, influenced our resentment towards each other. Of course, at the time we didn't realize these were important influences within our conflict. We just thought, "I'm right and Jessica/Bluma is the problem; if she would only stop being 'that way,' everything would be better."

As we began to explore how our parents influenced the way we saw each other and how we justified treating each other, we noticed that we each remembered very different versions of the same memories. For so many years, we fought, each believing that our version of the memories were right and that the other's was wrong. Here is one memory that we feel really shows how these parental relationships influenced our dynamic, and how in our different recollections of the same memory, we were both right - just approaching it from a different angle.

We'll start with Bluma's recollection.

It was a hot and dry Texas summer day whose scorching heat could only be cured by immersing yourself into a friend's pool's cool water, which was exactly what I'd done that afternoon. But now, with only a few hours before I met my girlfriends that evening, I had to face the bane of my existence and tame my chlorine-soaked mane of curls – a medusa-like sprawl of mixed blonde and brown spirals.

Freshly showered and wrapped in a towel, I stood before the bathroom mirror ready for battle - brush and hairdryer brandished like my own sword and shield - when suddenly, I saw Jessica fly in. Before I could even register what was happening, she'd ripped the dryer out of my hands and was beating me with it, screaming all the while like a possessed demon. I crumpled to the floor, shrinking my body into a ball to shield myself from the blows, as she pounded away. At 15, my older sister was smaller than me - 5 feet nothing and slight - but she had the strength of a 6-foot linebacker and didn't hesitate to attack me whenever she could. From her position looming above, armed with the dryer, I was helpless. This was nothing new: just my sister's latest strike in the longstanding terror campaign she'd been waging against me for as long as I could remember. Jessica terrified me. I'd lost count of the number of times she'd beat me up. When she flew into a rage, she was like a monster you could not reason with: no amount of pleading or placating would bring her to her senses. I was in a constant state of terror and apprehension, waiting for the next blow up. Worst of all, after each eruption, she expressed no remorse and expected me to simply forget. She'd even try to hug me, which I found confusing. She just wanted to move on, but I couldn't.

As Jessica hit me with the hairdryer, I screamed out in pain and terror and cried out for help. My mother was often my only line of defense against Jessica. I hardly ever got any time to her myself - she was always either working or helping Jessica with her homework, a process that could take hours because of her dyslexia - but I knew she preferred my company to Jessica's. We were so similar. I knew she was proud of my eloquence and thoughtfulness. We always teamed up for verbal volley. I was the one she confided in about her troubles with our dad. Thankfully, she came to my rescue. She yanked Jessica off me and assessed the damage. My face and back were covered in scratches. "Bluma, are you ok? Are you hurt?" she asked urgently. Then, more angrily, "Oh my God, Jessica! What have you done? What am I going to do with you? You always take it too far!"

Relief swept over me as I let my arms fall away from my face: the attack was finally over.

Now, here's what Jessica remembers of the same event.

It was late afternoon and I was watching TV in the living room when I heard my sister Bluma shout from the bathroom. I couldn't make out the exact words, but I felt my body tense. Bluma always monopolized the bathroom. She was self-conscious about her curly hair and not only took ages to straighten it, but flipped out if I did anything to disrupt the process. If I took a shower while she was in there and failed to completely shut the shower door, accidentally steaming up the room, which crimped her hair, she'd fly into a screaming, monster rage. And it wasn't just her hair. It felt like every little thing I did set her off. She was probably criticizing something I had supposedly done, again. And I'd had enough of her abuse for the day.

I marched into the bathroom. "What's your fucking problem?" I asked. Bluma yelled back, "Nothing, idiot. Can't you see

I'm doing my hair? Get the fuck out of here." Her voice and gaze dripped with condescension. Bluma had shamed me all week, and this was the last strike. I snapped.

I grabbed Bluma's hairdryer and screamed, "Shut the fuck up! Stop being so mean to me! I fucking hate you!" And then I beat the shit out of her.

It felt like an out-of-body experience as my rage took over. I screamed and pummeled my sister until I felt myself being pulled off, and heard our mom's voice yell, "Jessica, stop it right now! You always take it too far and make things worse." I let my arms hang at my sides, my breathing labored. I could barely even hear her, my adrenaline was so high. "You really did it this time, didn't you," our mom continued. "Why do you always have to be so horrible to your sister? You're so aggressive."

Bluma, standing next to our mom, chimed in. "Jessica's so horrible! She just came in here while I was drying my hair and attacked me for no reason. She's crazy." A sense of injustice rippled through me. I wanted to respond, explain how Bluma had provoked me, how she always engineered my outbursts then hid under a mantle of innocence. "Mom, Bluma started..." I tried to carry on, but the words wouldn't come. "She just..." I tried again, but I could see my mom's impatience and felt my frustration surge, which made talking even more difficult. Our mom sent me to my room. Through the door, I heard her consoling Bluma.

This was my life: a constant battle to protect myself. I was the only one who cared about me. I was all alone. My sister may have been younger than me by three years, but she regarded and treated me like an inferior. And our mom always, always sided with her. She never listened when I tried to explain that Bluma had started our fights with me. I was always at fault. In my mom's eyes, I was the difficult one. She made no secret of the fact that she preferred Bluma to me. They were a duo, and I was on my own, so I had to learn to stand up for myself.

These versions of the same memory, as different as they are, are both completely true. They show why we felt so afraid of and hurt by each other. You can see the pattern of behavior we learned from our dad - the eruption followed by no apology or resolution. We both felt tortured by each other. Neither of us could understand how the other ticked, and why they behaved the way they did. We took up different weapons - Bluma her words, and Jessica her fists - but the underlying feelings of confusion and pain were the same. What was different was how our mom reacted to us, and how that informed how we reacted to each other.

As you can see in our painful memory, our mom's immediate response, her gut feeling, was to protect Bluma. In a way, that makes sense: she's a mother who tunes into trouble when she hears one of her children screaming in pain and, arriving on the scene, sees her child crumpled on the floor in the fetal position, while her other child is hitting her. In our mom's mind, the situation was clear: Bluma was the victim, and Jessica was the aggressor. She probably didn't have the bandwidth to probe deeper: she was a busy mom, active on boards and charitable organizations whose responsibilities extended beyond the home. Being a mom is taxing, especially when you have four kids - including two at each other's throats all the time. Plus, most of our fights at this point ended with Jessica hitting Bluma, so this is what she was used to seeing.

What she didn't see was how Jessica's seemingly disproportionate reaction came from a deep place of feeling repeatedly unseen and unheard.

Our mom's reaction reinforced a narrative that fuelled resentment between us: that Jessica was the aggressor - the enemy, the black sheep, the outcast - and Bluma was the protected - our mom's ally, her favorite, the righteous one. Remember the story we told in Chapter 1, when our mom got mad at Jessica for picking up baby Bluma out of her crib to show her off to our parents' guests? The same message was being communicated over and over again - that Jessica's unbridled energy was a threat to Bluma. The more our mom made Jessica feel this way, the more she acted out in an effort to defend herself.

What we couldn't understand back then was that we were both contributing to this cycle of abuse and violence. There was no "perpetrator" or "victim." We played both parts. What we needed was someone to sit us down and help us see that. We needed an adult to gently and kindly tell us it wasn't acceptable for either of us to say hurtful things or hit each other. We needed to learn how to communicate and mutually respect each other. Our mom was doing her best, but focusing on Jessica's part and Bluma's pain made us double down in our belief that we were each being wronged. Bluma felt wronged because of the repeated physical attacks by Jessica; Jessica felt wronged because our mom repeatedly singled her out as the problem and rejected her.

Our mom was setting the barometer: through her actions she was showing us that what Bluma did was "less wrong" than what Jessica did, that Bluma could get away with saying hurtful things to Jessica, and that Jessica would get in trouble when she responded. Bluma learned just how far she could go without getting in trouble, and Jessica knew she'd get in trouble anyways. So the fighting never stopped, and the repairs never came. Wash, rinse, repeat.

This is true for so many families. How many times have you heard someone laugh and say, "So and so got away with murder in our family!" Siblings keenly remember how their parents were harder or gentler on one kid but not the other, or expected more or less from one kid than the other. This can affect them on a deep level. They may even feel that their parents love them less than other siblings.

We want to be clear: parents are not villains for treating their kids differently. They have a lot to contend with: each child has their own personality and develops independently. It makes sense that parents will treat each child differently depending on each of their abilities and temperaments, and as they match or mismatch with their parents. However, parents having a favorite can likely make one child feel rejected and less loved than their brother or sister. In 2005 (and replicated in 2016), the Journal of Family Psychology published a study showing that out of 768 parents surveyed, 74 percent of mothers and 70 percent of fathers admitted to having a favorite child. Parents may not be entirely aware they're favoring one sibling over another, or understand how it is affecting their children's relationships, and may even believe their children don't know. Or sometimes, they're up front and loud and proud about it, stating publicly who their favorite child is, and who isn't. This kind of favoritism is normalized in our popular culture, in the TV shows and movies we watch. We both watched Netflix' "Dead to Me" and saw how one character acknowledged his twin brother was their mom's favorite and he was his family's "Black Sheep," delivered as an innocuous punchline. This is so common.

Our parents *easily* recalled the various sibling dynamics within their own families of origin ("This one was the troublemaker, this one was the comic relief, this one was the goody-two-shoes, this one was the favorite") since these experiences were the undergird for what molded them. Like mirror corners cascading to infinity, the transgenerational history that flows through us, and the legacy burdens that get visited upon us, carry back from one generation to the next.

When people have kids, they bring a lifetime of experiences to their parenting. The books they've read, the advice they were given and - most of all - the parenting they received, all form the basis for their own parenting style and decisions. Legacy burden refers to the idea that parents pass down their unresolved issues to their children, consciously or not. Put simply, if a person experienced trauma because they felt unloved by their parent or parents, they're likely to pass down that same dynamic, and, unwittingly, make their own child feel unloved.

This happened in our family. We have to climb a few generations up our family tree to explain.

Our maternal great-great-grandmother was a gifted medical student, trained as a midwife, who fell in love with a man her parents deemed unacceptable, and was forced to marry a much older man they regarded as worthy, but whom she did not love. They moved from Russia across the world to the United States. There, she poured her energy into political activism and campaigned for women's suffrage. We love her for that. She had two kids, a daughter and a son. The girl - our great-grandmother - was incredibly bright and managed to get into Columbia University's College of Dental Medicine at a time when women hardly ever advanced that far academically. She was one of the first female dentists in the country. Our great-great-grandparents agreed to send her to school on the condition that she would apprentice her brother into dentistry (he was not accepted to medical school). This was quite common for the times, but it may have set the stage for feelings of inadequacy, superiority/inferiority, and favoritism between them. It could have also created a feeling of loyalty and resilience too. Our great-grandmother continued her career as a dentist throughout her life, honing in on the women's rights her own mother forged. We love her for that too. She married and had two girls, Estelle (our grandmother) and Vera. Our great-grandmother doted on Vera, the slender second; our grandfather adored our grandmother, the curvy first. When Estelle, our grandmother, had two daughters of her own, she subconsciously reproduced a similar favoritism. She doted on our aunt, and was incredibly harsh with our mom, the younger of the two daughters. In fact, many times the family referred to our mother as Vera's daughter, since she mirrored her physique and mild nature.

That brings the timeline to us. As we've already pointed out, our mom felt a clear affinity with Bluma and not Jessica. Perhaps she remembered how, as the second child, she was not as valued as the first, and unconsciously related more to Bluma as another second child. Maybe she wanted to course correct and make sure her second child didn't feel rejected like she had.

In each generation, one sibling was "programmed" to feel hurt and jealous of their other sibling for receiving more attention from one of their parents. This is something that happens in a lot of families. The tragedy of this is that no one is doing this on purpose. It's all happening on a subconscious level. Our mom didn't realize she was reinforcing a dynamic where one of us felt favored and the other felt neglected, just like her mother didn't realize she was doing the same.

We've focused mainly on our mom's family history because most of these complex dynamics impacted mother-daughter and sister-sister relationships, and that ended up forming a big part of our inheritance. We don't want to leave our dad out, though. He was also handed a big, complicated family history that affected him deeply.

When our father was two years old, an only child, our grandfather had volunteered to serve in WWII as a Gunner in B-17s, while our grandmother joined the Calutron Girls of Oak Ridge, TN, the famous location of the Manhattan Project. Our dad moved in with our great-grandmother in Middlesboro, KY, and she raised him until he was six. He was reunited with his parents after the war, but having missed out on those precious early years together, coupled with our grandfather's shell shock and our grandmother's ambivalent return to housewifery, it was hard for all of them to bond. It became even harder when his parents added two brothers to their family. Our father felt like an outsider to this "new" family. Did this legacy burden of being the eldest child and feeling like an outsider factor into Jessica's feeling of being an outsider within our own family?

We wondered how these traits and feelings get "passed down." What was contributing to the repetition of acceptance or rejection of parent to child? Was it nature? Nurture? How could we stop the cycle? To understand, we started by looking at the beginning. In our case, our mom was not consciously withholding affection from Jessica. A combination of legacy burdens and circumstances conspired against her. It was only recently that Jessica found out our mom did not breastfeed her as a baby, and exclusively breastfed her three other children. According to Dr. C. Sue Carter's research on oxytocin and pair bonds, breastfeeding is a primary source of oxytocin release for both a mother and her baby. Oxytocin is a small protein-like molecule that acts as a messenger in the nervous system, helping brain cells communicate, and influences mood, pain, and stress. Doctors told our mom not to breastfeed; it was a popular medical trend at the time to bottle feed with formula. Now we know that breastfeeding is a valuable bonding experience. This early release of oxytocin, involved in social connection and bonding, is not just biological, but a cornerstone for forming lasting emotional bonds, and highlights the importance of such moments—or their absence—on relationships. This may have contributed to our mom's difficulty to feel close to Jessica, a struggle she didn't experience with Bluma or our other siblings, all of whom she breastfed. Bonding without breastfeeding happens all the time. We both used a hybrid of breast/bottle feeding with our own children. Still, we wondered if this may have been one piece to our struggle-puzzle.

Human touch is as important to babies as food. This was proven by an extraordinary experiment conducted by psychologist Harry Harlow, who took infant monkeys away from their biological mothers and exposed them to two objects designed to serve as surrogate mothers: one made out of wire, the other made out of soft terry cloth. Harlow placed milk bottles alternatively with either set of surrogate mothers and watched what happened. He found that the baby monkeys spent significantly more time with the terry cloth mothers, even when they didn't have milk. They would drink milk from the wire mothers, then run back to the terry cloth mothers to cling to them.

Touch - like being held by parents and feeling their warmth - is vital to humans' healthy development because it's what makes us feel safe. One of the first things we do as human beings is to develop skills that allow us to evaluate what is safe and what is risky. As a species, that's how we have learned to survive. Feeling safe or feeling scared are our two basic modes. They're two states we have right out of the womb, before we feel any other kind of more complex emotion. We experience these two states deep in our nervous system. They're controlled by the vagus nerve.

The vagus nerve is located at the base of your brain, and it's the longest nerve in your body; it reaches down to your upper diaphragm organs (your heart, kidneys, liver, stomach, spleen and lungs) and all the way up your neck and into the muscles around your mouth, your ears and your eyes. You know how, when you're angry or scared, your eyes narrow and your pupils dilate? That's your vagus nerve preparing you to detect all signs of danger. And when you're happy or calm, your eyes open up wide and your pupils relax? That's your vagus nerve telling you it's safe; you can get curious and have fun. This innate response is raw and broad. Within the first year of being born, as you develop this physiological response, you look to your parents for guidance on how to interpret social situations and classify them as either safe or risky. We do this by picking up on the energy around us. We feel our parents' reactions to situations. We look to them for answers to questions like, "Is this person a friend or foe?" "How far is far enough?" "What's going to happen next?" "Is this good or bad?" If your parents show you they feel at ease and content, you learn to interpret this energy as 'everything is fine'. If, on the other hand, they show you they feel stressed or unhappy, you deduce 'something's not right'. You learn to frame social situations accordingly. This is the birth of the barometer we talked about at the beginning of this chapter. These early experiences teach us to measure our experiences using this as our gauge, because our bodies can detect risk or safety before our brains know what it means.

In fact, research shows that this all starts even before we're born. If a man or woman has an extreme physical or psychological event, it can leave a 'chemical mark' on the genes they pass on. For example, studies of people who suffered starvation showed metabolic changes in their offspring. Simply put, their future generations had higher rates of obesity, diabetes and cardiovascular disease, likely because a gene involved in burning the body's fuel was "warned" by their predecessor's trauma and turned off. When a pregnant woman has a traumatic experience and her stress levels are high, this elevation can impact the fetus' neurobehavioral development. In fact, some studies show it actually ages the fetus, so that when the baby is born, the placenta's "age" is older than the baby! That's why prenatal environments are so important for healthy fetal development. The hormones mothers pass on to their babies when they're pregnant are like a message telling them, "Hey kiddo, I'm getting you ready for what you're going to face when you come out the gate. You've got to be prepped and ready for this very stressful environment you're about to face." The present stressor facing the parent

> ***Deep dive***: The energy we're picking up on is actually hormones. The primary and most fundamental stress hormone in mammals is cortisol. And cortisol levels in our body are mediated by something called glucocorticoid receptors (GRs). The more GRs you have, the better you are at managing stress, because they calibrate/balance between your resiliency and vulnerability to fearful situations. And one of the major ways you acquire more GRs is through maternal care. Loving and nurturing contact with our primary caregiver(s) when we are babies affects the cognitive development of GRs, and sets the stage for how well we will manage stress for the rest of our lives.

becomes archived into the babies 'files', and voilà, they have their first legacy burden.

What's happening is that all this stress or trauma is getting passed down through something called epigenetics. You can see the word "gene" in "epigenetics." Genetics (DNA) are hardcoded and cannot change. Epigenetics, on the other hand, are proteins that wrap around genes and turn them on or off, deciding whether the gene gets expressed or silenced. Think of genes like a line of permanent marker, and epigenetics like pencil marks you can draw or erase.

So if your DNA is fixed but the on/off switch is reversible, how can you control the changes? In the simplest terms: by changing your environment or your behavior. A neuroscientist named Frances Champagne conducted experiments with rats to prove this. She observed two broad categories for how rat mothers repeatedly nurtured their young. In one group, the mothers spent a lot of time Licking and Grooming their pups (High LG). In the other group, the mothers did not Lick or Groom their pups very much (Low LG). Generation after generation, the High LG pups who were Licked and Groomed a lot by their mothers grew up to become leaders of the pack; they displayed confidence and resilience, didn't become overwhelmed by stressful situations - like finding their way out of a maze, and quickly and easily calmed down after a stressor. Plus, they were highly social. Meanwhile, the Low LG pups who were Licked and Groomed less by their mothers developed in less healthy ways. They grew up to be much more prone to anxiety, depression, obesity, addiction, and they struggled to reduce tension following a negative event, making them more isolated.

On the surface, this difference between the two groups looked like a difference in genetic makeup. But then Champagne decided to try something. She cross-fostered them. She had High LG mothers foster Low LG pups, and Low LG mothers foster High LG pups. And something amazing happened. The Low LG pups fostered by the High LG mothers developed the qualities of High LG pups (social, leaders, resilient), and they became High LG mothers themselves; and the High LG pups fostered by the Low LG mothers developed the qualities of Low LG pups (anxious, depressed, dysregulated), and became Low LG mothers, too. And this change lasted for generations as well, upwards of 30! Champagne realized that this nurturing behavior wasn't hard coded into the rats' DNA. It could be altered by changing the behavior and the environment the pups were exposed to early in life. Their maternal care affected changes in the pups' organic, cognitive development that set a trajectory for them for the rest of their lives–and set a stable, repeating pattern for their generations to follow. It came down to epigenetics–the power to change was something that could be controlled.

As humans, we also have this remarkable ability to break cycles. If our mothers, often through no direct fault of their own, struggled to make us feel as safe, nurtured and accepted as we needed when we were babies, we can course correct when we have children of our own, and alter the trajectory for generations to come.

Moms are not created out of thin air; they're trained. We want to give mothers the knowledge and support they need to bond with their babies, and hopefully limit the burdens being passed down to children and grandchildren, as has happened with so many of us. Whether you are a mother yourself, hoping to become one, or married to or friends with one, we want this book to help to create a new world in which we all contribute to helping kids become more resilient human beings. We want all children to grow up with the confidence to chase their dreams, with peace of mind, heart and spirit, and the best chance to build happy, healthy families. And that starts with early, healthy, loving and nurturing relationships with their parents - and their siblings.

How we are nurtured to see risk or safety, to cope with stress and regulate our emotions, impacts how we behave socially. And these styles get reinforced in our families, with our siblings. Jessica and Bluma thought it would always be "this way", we now know it can be altered. There is more hope with more understanding.

Chapter recap:

- Your parents directly and indirectly impact your sibling relationship by showing you conflict-resolution models and by acting as barometers that tell you what kinds of behaviors you can and can't get away with with your sibling.

- Parents' acceptance and/or rejection of their children has important developmental consequences. Children who feel accepted by and safe with their parents will learn to better manage stress than children who feel rejected by and unsafe with their parents. This will impact how comfortable children are with other people and how confident they feel to pursue their dreams.

- Because of transgenerational trauma, or legacy burdens, parents can pass down unhealthy sibling dynamics to their children. By understanding this legacy, you can take actions to break the pattern and help the next generation of siblings see and treat each other as allies instead of competitors fighting for their parents' love and attention.

CHAPTER 4

How Your Sibling Relationship Affects You And Your Future Relationships

People say you "marry" your parents. We say you marry your siblings, too.

Often, you search for romantic partners who remind you of your parents, since parents are the earliest models of love, care and security. That can be a good or bad thing. Imagine a child who grew up feeling accepted, loved and supported by their parents - whose brain developed to perceive safety and risk accurately and, accordingly, learned mechanisms to cope with stress. That child will probably seek out romantic relationships that make them feel just as grounded. Now think of a child who grew up feeling afraid of, or confused and rejected by their parents - whose brain struggled to differentiate between safety and risk and, therefore, did not develop healthy stress coping mechanisms. That child may seek out relationships that mimic that dynamic, since that will be the story they are familiar with. This is attachment theory in a nutshell - the now wildly popular theory discovered by psychologists John Bowlby and Mary Ainsworth. Essentially, you are attracted to what's familiar to you. And that doesn't mean that what you're attracted to is healthy.

It's only recently that we fully realized we both married men who evoked many of the same feelings we experienced at home with our parents. We chose these men, who we believed could provide us the stability we missed from our chaotic upbringing. It was only years into our commitments that we realized that what we thought were safe harbors - steady ground on which to build a new life - were actually much more akin to the rocky shores of our youth. Deep down, we didn't feel liked or celebrated by our partners. We didn't feel accepted for who we were. If all human relationships are defined by how accepted or rejected we feel by another person, as we've discussed throughout this book, then our marriages made us feel stuck on the far side of rejection in this continuum. We didn't feel fully loved, seen or respected by our spouses, just like we hadn't with our parents: Bluma, vis-a-vis our dad, and Jessica, vis-a-vis our mom.

And as we embarked on our healing journey together, we realized something else. We'd also sought out partners who reminded us of each other.

As your peers from your earliest age - the humans you play and fight with, probably more than your parents - your siblings are the ones who teach you how to behave in your future relationships. But because you're all kids, you don't know what you're doing! You're not experts on best practices in human interactions. That's why you need good models. As we explained in Chapter 2, sibling relationships undergird how we learn to operate socially in the world. If you learn to handle friction with your sibling by throwing things or threatening, you're hard-wiring yourself to cope with conflict though outward aggressive behavior.

Since we both felt a huge amount of injustice in our home - Bluma, because Jessica attacked her without warning; Jessica, because Bluma shattered her with verbal jabs and never faced consequences - we harnessed the depths of our powerlessness and sadness and unleashed them on each other as anger.

This whole cocktail of emotions - these feelings of neglect and anger - waltzed right into our marriages. Today, we realize we married people who made us feel the way we made each other feel: small and unvalued. We married people who did not want us to shine, who were so

> ***Deep Dive***: although there is a trend in therapeutic circles that beating up a pillow or screaming your anger out is helpful in soothing your feelings, it actually is NOT the case. It creates a stimulus-response pattern where your body expects that when presented with a negative situation (stimulus), you will respond with an outburst (hitting, screaming, etc.). Even if it is cathartic in the moment, it is not helpful long-term. And that pattern will follow you into marriage. You may no longer throw your toys or threaten to uninvite people to your birthday party, but you may struggle to settle the rage and frustration that gets triggered and not be sure how to handle friction.

uncomfortable with our light that they extinguished it as often as they could.

We married the parent we struggled with, and the sibling we struggled with. Bluma married our dad and Jessica. Jessica married our mom and Bluma.

Now, we want to be clear: fixing your sibling relationship **does not** mean your romantic relationship will fall apart. It takes two people to participate in a *happy* or unhappy marriage. While we put a lot of energy and effort into our respective marriages, continually reading books and seeking counseling to try to resolve perpetual issues, our partners appeared to only want us to change - to stop "wanting more" - and did not seem to want to develop and expand themselves. Healing our relationship as siblings - and both deciding that doing so was a worthwhile investment of our time and energy - proved that healing a broken bond takes a great amount of work and will. In our cases, after 16 and 23 years of marriage, healing our sibling relationship confirmed to us that our marriages had never really worked. It didn't cause our divorces.

In fact, we firmly believe that understanding the root cause of your sibling hostility and fixing your relationship can help you improve the quality of your romantic relationship, or, if you don't have one, can help you choose a good partner. Healing your sibling relationship helps you seek out people who respond to who you are now, not the role you played back then. We want you to thrive in your romantic relationships, and beyond. Your sibling relationship is the model on which you build your future relationships with the people closest to you, from your partners to your friends to your business partners. Becoming aware of and addressing the patterns that plagued you in your sibling relationship equips you with the best tools to build lasting and meaningful bonds.

At heart, what we're talking about here is building community. As we established in Chapter 2, you're wired to be a "we," not a "me." We thrive in this world by surrounding ourselves with people who lift us up and make us feel seen. The husbands, wives or partners, friends and associates we choose to include in our lives are the primary pillars of our own communities. They are our support networks. They pick us up when we fall, and celebrate us when we succeed. So it's vitally important we choose people we can rely on. And one of the primary ways we learn how to choose and attract the right people, and create fruitful bonds with them, is through our experiences in our childhood home, with our siblings. Those are our very first community.

Because we both instinctively knew our homes had not provided us a good, supportive sense of community and that we, as sisters, were not allies we could count on, we sought community out elsewhere. Yet because we did not know what a good community model looked like, we struggled to find groups of people with whom we could truly be ourselves. This search for community - for a space in which to be our authentic selves - is a defining, lifelong pursuit for all of us. Healing your sibling relationship is key to achieving this fundamental goal.

We want to tell you about our individual experiences trying to build communities; the challenges we faced, and how healing our relationship has utterly transformed our ability to both gravitate towards and attract people who bring out the best in us. As you read along, we'd like you to reflect on your own experiences: the friend groups, partners and overall communities you've had at different stages of your life, how they made you feel, and whether some of the dynamics within them remind you in any way of your relationship with your sibling.

Throughout elementary, middle and high school, Bluma was devoted to a group of friends. "The girls" were an inseparable unit known throughout their schools' halls. From them, she learned how to be a considerate friend; how to prioritize and make efforts toward meeting a friend's needs and preferences, from favorite foods to gift-giving, and above all, how to be loyal. At times, her loyalty felt one-sided, and while she was willing to confront conflict - never hesitating to march right up to a friend and address an issue or injustice - it also made her feel like she constantly had to lobby for their love and acceptance, or risk losing it. Her fears weren't unfounded. On several occasions they ghosted Bluma without giving her any real reason as to why, and then, with the same lack of logic or explanation, they welcomed her back into the fold.

Each time, Bluma felt relief, then dread that it would happen again. It wasn't unlike how she sometimes felt at home, where Jessica would attack her without provocation (how it felt to Bluma), then expect them both to move on, without any explanation. Those cycles also made Bluma toggle between relief and dread. Because Jessica was her older sister, Bluma couldn't help but want to be loved by her, to be celebrated and admired by her the way she looked up to Jessica. But because that felt out of reach, Bluma sought out those feelings of connection and support from her friends. When they, too, made her feel unwanted, the lesson she took away was that she had to adapt to them; she had to fit her circle into their square in order not to lose them. If she was going to have relationships, she had to twist and shape herself into what others could manage and tolerate. This was often an uncomfortable and isolating experience, but she felt like she had no other choice. The girls were the trophy, proof that she was lovable, valuable. And if she could win them over, she would be accepted; she would be enough.

Part of what was going on was that Bluma - as a kid growing up in a chaotic household, afraid her dad might come home in a foul mood and rage, or that her sister might swing a punch at her unexpectedly - needed reassurance and validation. Our mom would not stand up to our dad and only yanked Jessica off of Bluma if she caught them fighting, which happened only after Jessica had already thrown a punch. Bluma needed to feel part of a tribe that made her feel safe and OK, and she found that with the girls. It was an understandable response to a stressful situation. But the problem was that by continually seeking reassurance from others, Bluma developed a coping mechanism, outsourcing her sense of wellbeing and safety to others, instead of drawing it from within herself. Looking for reassurance from a friend group who didn't fully accept her was a helpful, adaptive response for a problem in the moment, but one that became an unhelpful, maladaptive habit over time. As an adult, Bluma felt a growing reluctance to squeeze her circle into the girls' square. So, she looked for another space into which she could more comfortably fit herself.

Bluma began exploring her spirituality and dove deep into her Jewish roots. There she found a welcoming community that provided a wonderful sense of closeness, structure and wellbeing. Bluma loved the intellectual pursuit of delving into *Halacha*, Jewish law. It was a blueprint for life. Every detail was considered and determined, from what to eat to how to act. Life was choreographed in a way that gave Bluma a sense of stability and hope. The limits were liberating. She no longer felt lost or confused. But over the years, she found herself bumping up against barriers around just how much she could be herself. She struggled to find her balance in a culture that both celebrates an educated and outspoken woman, and also values a woman's modesty and reserve. This push and pull in opposite directions seemed untenable. It felt like on the inside, her engine revved, but she had to contain the motion and appear neutral on the outside, lest she risk rejection for non-conforming (which not only risked her acceptance as a *religious* woman, but also put at risk the equilibrium within the community). Again, she felt like a circle in a world of squares. Again, she was looking for an external source to define her worth, to confine her role, and to approve of her so she would be accepted and safe.

When, together, Jessica and Bluma began this process of healing our past sibling relationship, Bluma finally started feeling a sense of clarity and closure vis-à-vis "the girls" and the divergence that had come to define their friendship. She also began to discover how to balance the growing need for diversity in her Jewish life. As we progressed in our healing, she felt that old need for reassurance melt into a deeper appreciation for who she was. "Fitting in" felt like a fool's errand, and she began to embrace the parts of herself she had tried to keep quiet. This, in turn, expanded her ability to accept others, too - to see more of the good and beauty in them.

Jessica, on her end, had in many ways the opposite experience. Feeling like an outlier at home, rejected by our mom and the tight group Bluma and our other siblings formed, taught her to be a fighter - to take no shit from anyone and never back down. Because she felt unseen and unheard by our family, she developed coping mechanisms to make sure they couldn't ignore her. This often took the form of interruptions. She figured, if her family was not going to pay attention to her, if they were going to make her feel excluded from their conversations, she'd find a way to make them shut up and stop whatever they were doing. It worked. And it became an automatic response for her when she wanted people to see her, in and out of her family. The problem, of course, is that interrupting people is disruptive, or rude. Like Bluma looking for validation from her group of friends, what started as an adaptive response for Jessica quickly became a maladaptive practice. And this need to be heard took on a life of its own. Despite her tiny frame, Jessica got into fights with girls twice her size in high school. She was fearless and intimidating, and she was popular: a star on the swim team, she drank with her teammates before practice and collected a string of besotted boyfriends who went out of their way to buy her gifts. But she struggled to make a close group of friends. She was charismatic and compelling but inspired fear, like a mob boss at the top of their game. It was often a lonely place to be.

It wasn't until she discovered Dale Carnegie's teachings at 19 that she felt a real sense of community for the very first time. She felt embraced and championed by a group of people bonded by the same values and beliefs. She learned to be generous with praise, to be genuinely interested in other people, and to quickly acknowledge her own mistakes. After two decades of constantly fending for herself, she melted into the kindness that surrounded her at last. The Carnegie courses she took on and off for 10 years gave her the structure and feedback she needed to connect with her peers, but she couldn't stay there forever. When she stopped attending classes and started making friends beyond the confines of this particular community - with people who didn't know or adhere to the Carnegie principles that had opened up a new world of empathy and respect for Jessica - old relationship patterns crept back in.

Many of the friendships Jessica made as an adult were based around competition and exhibiting competence. An entrepreneur, she was drawn to women in business; savvy professionals like herself with a knack for sales and negotiation. They encouraged each other professionally, but also sharpened each other's competitive edges, which occasionally came out as a certain meanness towards others. They fell into a set of roles that seemed to get them what they wanted, whether at business conferences or hotels: Jessica played "bad cop" while her friends got to play "good cop." Jessica would come out guns blazing, defending her friends when they got embroiled in disputes or demanding whatever she and her friends needed: the hotel suite they'd booked but which, at the last minute, had been given to someone else; access to a conference to which they were still on the waitlist. She was like a panther in stealth mode. Then, once whichever manager or gatekeeper they were dealing with was sufficiently frazzled, her friends could sweep in and act like the more reasonable, apologetic party, ready to compromise to settle the dispute. It was a method that worked and bonded Jessica to her friends. The lesson she learned was that people around her - her new communities - embraced her showing up aggressively. They expected her to be that way.

You see, however different our experiences, we were both struggling to find the right communities and to be accepted as the selves we wanted to be.

Within a few weeks of our sibling healing process, Jessica realized she no longer wanted to be her friends' panther. She quietly took some space from friends who celebrated this side of her. She realized that the sense of competition she'd always felt around them reminded her of how she'd felt around Bluma, and how this need to feel seen, to be valued, and to not be taken advantage of was creating toxic dynamics. Now she seeks support rather than competition in her friendships.

Healing our relationship has opened up a new world of nurturing relationships.

In order to start to cultivate flourishing communities, we had to process our past sibling trauma. Remember the Zeigarnik Effect we discussed in Chapter 1? The phenomenon that allows your brain to hold on to information for as long as it needs while it works out a solution to a problem? Unprocessed negative or traumatic experiences - like painful sibling memories - keep the Zeigarnik Effect active. As long as your painful memories are left unprocessed, abandoned in the past, exiled in your mind, your brain is stuck in a loop - trying to understand your pain and find a solution to relieve it. It's constantly ruminating, cycling through the mind, intruding into your thoughts, sabotaging your wellbeing, all while making you believe it's protecting you from harm. It's not.

Our unprocessed, negative childhood experiences warped the way we saw the world and our roles and relationships in it.

It's only by processing them that we can finally get some clarity on why and how we developed maladaptive coping mechanisms, and how those influenced the kinds of people we attracted and chose to surround ourselves with.

In our case, the stress we experienced as young children limited our ability to assess risk and danger properly, which in turn restricted our capacity to bond with others in a way that was fully constructive. Our vagus nerve - the part of the ancient brain we discussed in Chapter 2 that assesses risk and safety - perceived so much risk in our formative years that we grew into people who were primed to sense danger, even in places where it wasn't actually lurking. That, in turn, made us respond to this perceived danger in the only ways we knew how - often, by getting dysregulated, disproportionately angry and defensive. And we subconsciously continued to seek out people who made us feel that way because that was what was familiar to us. We were stuck in a vicious cycle: we'd seek out communities that allowed us to play out our role or reminded us of the stress we'd inflicted on each other at home, and consequently, we would end up in situations where our brains were continuously switching on our fight/flight/freeze modes.

It felt like it was out of our control. And it was - until we learned how to take back the reins.

Think of your vagus nerve response - that unconscious command to fight, flight or freeze - like the weather. You can't control it. If it's going to rain, it's going to rain. But you can prepare for it. You can bring an umbrella. You can understand what's happening to your body when you feel yourself getting triggered or stressed, and you can calm your system down. You can self-soothe your body and your mind and teach it that you're OK. That there's no reason to panic because you've got this. That is exactly what we're going to teach you to do in the next chapter. It might seem hardwired right now, but we promise, it's just like riding a bike. Once you get it, it'll be easier and easier to keep going. You will feel more in control. And that, we promise, will change your life!

This whole process of reflecting and understanding your past, as well as learning to control your stress responses, is what finally turns OFF the Zeigarnik Effect. And by freeing your mind of the continual churn, you suddenly have the space and the energy to focus on moving forward constructively. You can finally build a meaningful community, starting with your sibling, and moving on to your romantic partners, friendships, business associates, and anyone else you choose to have in your life.

We can't tell you how excited we are to begin this transformative journey with you. So let's get started.

Chapter recap:

- You are attracted to what feels familiar to you, but what's familiar is not always healthy. If, as a child, you felt unloved or neglected by your parents and siblings, you are likely to seek out romantic partners who make you feel that way too.

- Your unprocessed, negative childhood experiences warp the way you see the world and your roles and relationships in it, and prime you to perceive more risk and danger in it than there really is. By processing your past, you can finally get some clarity on why and how you react to people a certain way - whether defensively or fearfully - and you can teach your body and mind to better manage stress.

- You can't control your feelings of stress or anger, but you can teach yourself to control your reactions to them. This is what will make you feel in control and help you build positive, nurturing relationships and feel part of a community in which you are your true, authentic self.

CHAPTER 5

Getting Started: Emotional Regulation

Now that you know why sibling relationships can fail and why it's so important to restore them, you're ready to embark on your own healing journey. But first, we want you to feel prepared for the unexpected feelings, worries or difficulties you may encounter on your path. In this chapter, we'll explain some of the measures we've incorporated into our process to make sure you feel secure and, if you start feeling overwhelmed, how you can find your center. This chapter is all about emotional regulation.

Simply put, emotional regulation is the practice of controlling your emotions instead of having them control you. To understand what emotional regulation is, it might be easier to start by giving you examples of emotional dysregulation. Imagine a toddler having a meltdown. You see a 4-year-old screaming and crying in the supermarket, lying face down on the floor. They might have been hungry and tired, and suddenly the tiniest trigger - their mom refusing to buy them a lollipop - set off a totally disproportionate reaction to this small frustration. That's dysregulation.

You probably don't have supermarket meltdowns, but now think of the last time you were coming home late after a long, tiring day at work and were really hoping your partner - who'd already missed a few of their turns making dinner that week - would have cooked something. You walk in and don't smell anything. Then you see them lounging on the couch. And they ask you what's for dinner. You throw your bag on the ground and yell at your partner, telling them they're useless and you hate them.

That's dysregulation again. We're not saying the anger is unjustified, but the response is a bit over the top and, more importantly, it's going to generate further frustration. Your partner is probably not going to react in a compassionate and understanding way. They're probably going to feel attacked and fight back. Everybody loses. So why did you react this way, even though in the back of your head, you knew the situation was only going to get worse? Here's what happened. That small trigger - realizing your partner had not cooked dinner as you had hoped - set off a whole cascade of bodily responses that sent your stress levels through the roof, in turn accelerating your heartbeat and breathing, all of which made you feel uncomfortably hot, panicked and seeing red. It also lassoed in other disappointments, expectations unmet and histories of feeling underappreciated. What was a 4 out of 10 stressor received a 9 out of 10 reaction.

When we emotionally regulate, we take stock of the trigger - whether that's our mom refusing to buy a lollipop or our partner not cooking dinner - and we don't let this domino effect of physiological responses lead us down a negative spiral. That's what allows us to approach conflict more calmly and productively.

Because there's no avoiding it – we all get triggered. And you will absolutely get triggered when you start healing your relationship with your sibling. Our program is about diving into your past to paint a brighter future, so you will have to revisit memories that may make you feel sad, or frustrated, or uncomfortable. And right now, that may sound like the last thing you want to do. You have a life to live! A job to do, maybe kids to raise, pets to care for, family and friends to support. You may think you simply don't have the time or the energy to deal with a bunch of overwhelming feelings that will plunge you into the past and get in the way of your day-to-day routine.

But we believe in you. We know it may seem impossible right now, with your past in your rearview mirror, but we're here to hold your hand through it. We've done it ourselves, and we've thought carefully about how to make sure you feel supported during this process. Once you're familiar with the steps, you'll not only see them as protective measures and boundaries, but you'll actually *enjoy* them. Think about it like starting meditation or yoga, or learning a new musical instrument or sport. The first few times you put time aside to do it, you might feel unsure and tentative about whether you're doing it right. But very quickly, once you get the hang of it, it feels fun, pleasurable, exciting even. And you can't wait to keep going. That's how you'll feel. **That's how it felt for us.**

Let's dive in.

Video calling

The first tool we want you to use to feel safe - to better emotionally regulate - is video calling. If you're scratching your head right now, that's OK; we realize this may sound counterintuitive. If the point of this experience is reconnecting with your sibling - establishing closeness - shouldn't you be physically close while you do it? Well actually, no! It's absolutely vital you do not start this work in person with your sibling. Even if you live in the same city - in the same neighborhood or on the same street - you must conduct your meetings through some kind of communication platform. Zoom, Google Meet, FaceTime, it doesn't matter. But you must communicate through a screen.

There are a few reasons for this. One is that you will feel more at home and in control if you are, literally, at home in your house, or wherever you feel most centered and protected. You can choose a room you feel good in - maybe your bedroom, office or living room. You can surround yourself with objects that are familiar to you, that make you feel like you. Traversing the landscape of your past sibling relationship can elicit destabilizing feelings. It can make you question the narrative you've written about yourself and force you to view yourself through a less flattering lens. You want to make sure you're in an environment that reminds you of why you love yourself and why other people love you, too.

Another reason we urge you to communicate through a screen is so that you can record your meetings. That way, if you wish, you can go back and watch yourself working through conflict. By viewing yourself like a character in a movie, you can see yourself more objectively and see how and why you're getting triggered and how and why you're responding the way you are. Also, the footage can serve as evidence. If you and your sibling have a disagreement over what happened during a call - you may remember a particular conversation differently - you can simply go back and rewatch it. That way, neither of you is beholden to one person's version of events. You have objective evidence. Full disclosure: of the thousands of hours on zoom together, we went back and watched 3 times. Knowing we could gave us a sense of protection to let go and lean in.

The final reason it is absolutely vital for you and your sibling to communicate through screens goes back to the vagus nerve. You remember this fundamental nerve in your body, the one that links your upper diaphragm to your eyes, mouth and nose? The one that triggers your ancient brain to switch on a fight, flight or freeze mode? Well, it's an incredibly perceptive mechanism that gets switched on by preverbal cues. It picks up on body movements, gestures, looks. If you are walking down the street and a person in front of you suddenly spins around, your vagus nerve may prompt you to flinch before you've even consciously realized you've done it. It registers that unexpected movement by another human as threatening and makes you react protectively. Your vagus nerve even picks up invisible cues like the hormones that other people release. If you're sitting in front of someone who is anxious or angry, and, as a result, is releasing cortisol or testosterone, your vagus nerve picks that up and sends a warning: there's something in your environment to feel scared or angry about. It tells you to get ready to fight, run away or play dead.

Think about it. Have you ever met a stranger and immediately had some kind of gut feeling about them? Felt some kind of push or pull towards them? Call it a spidey sense - when this happens, your two bodies are vibing, feeding off of and digesting all the hormones you're releasing. Your senses can be right or wrong - the person you initially thought you should be guarded against could end up being your best friend. It doesn't matter. The point is that our bodies perceive other bodies in ways we don't even consciously realize.

Well, if your body can gather information from a total stranger, just imagine how much information it can pick up from someone you have history with - like a sibling. The way they glance to the side, or hold their hands in their lap, or tense their shoulders, or even smile - you will know all of these expressions and gestures intimately and have an innate reaction to them. Your sibling might cock their head to the left, and to a stranger it might look like they're being thoughtful. But because you know them, and you've seen them pull this move on you time and time again, you "know" that what they're actually communicating to you right now is disinterest. Or superiority. Or doubt. And you'll immediately feel yourself respond with a cocktail of anger, sadness and frustration. Your vagus nerve has turned on your fight, flight or freeze switch.

Obviously, none of those switches are conducive to having a productive and calm conversation with your sibling. That's why it's incredibly difficult to rewire a relationship in person. You're getting triggered by all of this nonverbal, physiological communication.

So, thank God for screens! By video calling your sibling, you get to see them in a frame that only shows their head and part of their torso, and limits the environment to a 2D experience. You can't see what they're doing with their hands. They could be balled in a fist or fidgeting with a pen - things which, if you could see them, might lead you to a conclusion and make you think they were angry or distracted. But you can't see them doing that, so you're not going to feel

> ***Deep Dive***: we also have something called mirror neurons which mimic what we see, and influences how we feel, because we experience it as if it originated from within us. When we see someone lick their lips, and all of a sudden you feel your own tongue swiping your own lips:mirror neurons. Or, if someone is tightening their brows and getting upset, we can also mimic (mirror, reflect) those physiological responses and catch the feeling too.

triggered - and vice versa. If your sibling starts talking about a painful memory that brings you back to that point in time and reminds you of the hurt you felt, you can release some of the tension you might feel in your body by gripping the edge of your seat or squeezing a stress ball in your hand under your desk. Your sibling won't see it, or sense it, and won't be distracted from their narrative, and won't accuse you of reacting negatively to what they're saying. And voilà, you've just avoided a fight. It mitigates the propensity to fall into old habits that bring you back to your 6 or 8 or 10-year-old selves, and instead allows you to stay in adult mode long enough to experience the childhood memories differently.

By being in different locations, you also prevent your bodies from picking up on stress hormones that could signal threat or danger. Because even if you can hide your hands from your sibling while you squeeze them in frustration, you certainly can't stop your body from producing and releasing hormones. By not being in the same room, you avoid picking up on these additional triggers, since your vagus nerve isn't able to pick up the hormones through a screen.

Circumstance forced us to zoom when we started this process. We were already living on separate continents, and then a global pandemic forced us all to shelter in our homes. We had no other option but to video call each other. But we very quickly saw what an advantage this was. It suddenly didn't seem like a coincidence that every other time in the past we'd tried to make peace, we'd tried in person and failed. We were just too overwhelmed by each other's physical presence.

Video calling was a game changer. It was our first tool to help us emotionally regulate.

Right now you might be thinking to yourself, sure, a screen can stop you from seeing what your sibling is doing outside of the frame, and from sensing the hormones they're releasing, but it definitely won't stop you from hearing whatever triggering thing they have to say. What then?

You're 100% right. But the point isn't to block out all the triggers - it's to minimize the onslaught of them so you have a chance to deal with what the trigger is actually about, and not get diverted or absorbed by the static surrounding it. And that brings us to the next emotional regulation tool.

Breathing

It may sound too good to be true, but breathing deeply is another game changer. The reason why goes back to something called the Polyvagal Theory. This theory, which was introduced by psychologist and neuroscientist Dr. Stephen Porges, sets out that the only way any of us can change our vagus nerve reaction - that instruction to fight, freeze or run away - is through the breath. Breathing is a control system that operates automatically and unconsciously, just like our heart rate, digestion or sexual arousal. But unlike other automatic systems[4], breathing is the only one we can control. You can't stop your heart from beating or elect to pause your digestion, but you can slow down your breathing or speed it up. And by slowing down your breathing, you send a signal to your vagus nerve that you're not, actually, in danger. You don't need to fight, freeze or run away. You're safe. You're OK.

Revisiting your past with your sibling - remembering the fights and the feelings of conflict and hostility - can make you feel like you're experiencing those fights in the present, as you discuss them. Your vagus nerve may start to trigger the fight, flight or freeze mode - because that's what it did so often when you were a kid, and kept doing every time you and your sibling saw each other and fought again. It's a learned behavior. And your whole body instinctively thinks there's a threat. It wants to protect you. So it speeds up your heart and quickens your breathing to get you ready to fight or run away. It puts

---

[4] Autonomic Nervous System: the system that runs without our participation or control.

you in survival mode. Your executive functioning - the part of your brain that helps you stay constructive and creative in how you process conflict and problem solve - goes offline when we are in survival mode. We literally hear differently; we pick up different tones, and anticipate danger, so that what might be positive or neutral can be experienced as negative. But taking a deep, slow breath, and then another - and another - calms those reactions. Slow inhalations bring in hearty amounts of oxygen that help our blood flow; slow exhalations, slow down our heartbeat and bring us back to baseline. And this allows us to heal, restore and renew.

We had to learn to breathe through the experience. It wasn't easy, but the more we did it, the easier it became. And then something remarkable happened. Once we were comfortable breathing through conflict, and our bodies weren't focused on protecting us from danger, this space opened up in our minds, allowing us to look at our past conflicts with curiosity. Trips down memory lane stopped being traumatic. They started feeling interesting. Enlightening. Hopeful.

By breathing deeply and intentionally, you will feel this too.

Grounding

Grounding is a therapeutic technique that connects you to the earth. It's deceptively simple: you stand barefoot on the ground, feet hips-width apart, and feel yourself standing tall and strong, yet relaxed, anchoring the soles of your feet into the ground. You can do this inside your house or outside; it doesn't matter where. We like to imagine roots growing from our feet into the earth, connecting your body and soul to it. You close your eyes. And you breathe deeply as you focus your attention on the different parts of your body, starting with your toes and your feet, moving up to your ankles, then your legs, all the way up to the crown of your head.

In a matter of seconds, this powerful stance makes you feel fully connected. Your mind and body become one, and you become one with your surroundings. With the Earth. You feel empowered and in control.

Jessica learned about grounding when she went through her health odyssey. When she started working with a breathing expert and incorporated grounding into her daily routine, she began healing in huge leaps. She suggested we start our Zoom sessions by grounding together. We did, and immediately noticed how calming it felt, how peaceful, but also how connected it made us feel. By doing it together - even from a distance - we could feel ourselves synching up. It was as if our connection to the ground, to the earth, connected us too. Our roots were finding each other and growing intertwined. It was a beautiful way to begin each session.

By introducing all of these emotional regulation tools during our sessions, we were able to constructively revisit our pasts. And we soon realized their benefits reached beyond our Zooms.

It would have been spooky if it weren't so welcome, but we started synching up. We'd have similar interactions with strangers and acquaintances, or have similar thoughts and epiphanies as we went about our days. We'd realize it when we'd meet up to zoom. Jessica would start telling Bluma about a thought or experience she'd had that week, and Bluma would have to contain her excitement before shouting, "That happened to me too!" We also realized that we generally didn't feel as frustrated or annoyed by small things as much anymore. There's a narrow street in Bluma's neighborhood that should really be one way, but allows for traffic both ways. Bluma used to feel herself fuming when cars would rudely shove their way down the street without even trying to accommodate hers; it was a small thing, but it was enraging, and something that happened daily. But as she made progress with Jessica, she noticed that she stopped feeling as frustrated on that street. The sense of "injustice" and "lack of consideration" she projected onto the oncoming drivers softened. It just didn't make her feel that angry anymore. The same was true about other daily triggers. For Jessica, too.

Just like they did for us, the emotional grounding tools you'll use in this journey will resonate beyond and into your day-to-day life. We weren't joking: healing your sibling relationship will change your whole life.

And now, at last, it's time to dive into the deep end and begin healing your sibling relationship. You're ready for it, and we're right here with you. Let's go.

The 6 Steps to Healing:

Step 1: Create a New Contract

Step 2: Identify Your Archetypes

Step 3: Memory Sharing

Step 4: Learning To Move Through Conflict

Step 5: Cultural Fusion

Step 6: Managing Your Evolution (Wash, Rinse, Repeat)

CHAPTER 6

Step 1 - Create A New Contract

On the previous page, you read our six steps to healing. Though we've written them in chronological order, you'll find that some of these can overlap. You may still be working out your Archetypes as you Memory Share and Refine your Conflict Dialogue, for example, and that's completely fine. While we do ask you to complete each step, the order you do it in is up to you in however it makes sense in the context of your unique sibling dynamic.

Now let's jump in.

Your sibling dynamic operates within a culture that you and your sibling have created and refined over the years. We typically understand culture as a function of a large group of people - a country or region, or on a smaller scale, a corporation or school. But it applies just as well to families.

What is culture? It's a set of shared attitudes, values, goals, and practices that characterizes a group of people. Celebrating holidays, birthdays and anniversaries, teaching the importance of voting in elections, or volunteering time/donating money are examples of practices and values a family can instill in each member within its very own culture. The point is to cultivate unity through common understanding. And within your broader family culture, you and your sibling will have your own culture.

If you and your sibling are caught in a negative spiral, your culture has definitely gone off the rails. Your shared attitudes and values may be something along the lines of, "I must make myself heard because they don't listen," or "I must defend myself at all costs because they don't respect me," and your practices may involve instigating fights or using alienating behaviors.

That's why you have to commit to a new culture. And the best way to elucidate exactly what you would like this new culture to look like is by getting it down on paper. So Step 1 of the healing process is creating a contract to set out how you would like your new sibling culture to be.

At this point, we're not concerned about whether you and your sibling want to celebrate or skip birthdays as part of your new culture. What we do want you to fully embrace are a set of values we believe are absolutely vital to healing your relationship, as well as a series of practices to jumpstart this new understanding between you. The following is the new sibling contract we created for ourselves. We believe it contains the core tenets necessary to forging a new, loving and supportive connection between you and your sibling. We encourage you to use it as a guide to create your own.

The Contract

The Prime Directive:

Yes, you can call Nerd Alert: we have a trekkie among us. But just like the Starfleet's, your Prime Directive is a set of guiding principles you must wholly embrace as you reset your sibling dynamic. They are the following:

— Be a Witness: You commit to be a **witness** to who you were in your sibling's story, not yourself in your story. As you and your sibling dive into the past, you must give your sibling the time and the space to share their memories of how they felt and the role you played in their experience (pain, loss, hurt). Listen to them and accept that this IS their truth.

— Be Remorseful: You commit to be **remorseful**. Even if you don't yet agree or remember, you have to commit to owning the pain that you caused your sibling. Acknowledge that your sibling suffered, and your relationship with them suffered too.

— Be Forgiving: You commit to be **forgiving**. It is time to choose to release the hold this pain has had on you and your sibling. By forgiving your sibling, and yourself, you can finally move through the past, and into the future, together.

— Be Curious: You commit to be **curious.** Rather than getting defensive when your sibling shares their truth, listen and pay attention. Don't fall into THE default, vintage patterns; keep yourself in an active-listening and understanding-seeking mode.

- Be Compassionate: You commit to staying **compassionate**. It's an attitude, a posture and a lens that filters what you hear, what you see and how you feel. Being compassionate isn't "letting them off the hook"; it's allowing them to feel their pain and wishing them peace. It is literally the key for YOU to have peace, groundedness and grace.

- Seek Understanding: You commit to seek **understanding.** By keeping your focus in seek-mode, you shift from "I already know what you're gonna say" to "I want to know what you mean."

The Schedule:

You commit to a set time that you will video call each other every week. We recommend 2 times every week for 4 weeks, no less than 1 hour per call. We felt that 90 minutes was our sweet spot.

The Procedure:

- Shoot the shit: You start each meeting with a "Shoot the shit" update (chitchat). Set a timer and give yourselves 5-10 minutes each to simply tell each other about your current lives. You can talk about what's happened in the last few days, something going on at work or with your kids, or anything on your mind that isn't directly related to this process. Healing your adult sibling relationship includes both exploring the pain points from your past and who you've become as adults (and the important people and things that fill your life now). This gives you something to build from, gives you perspective on who your sibling is now (as opposed to the tainted version of them you've carried in your mind), and helps you know and care about them.

— Grounding: Before diving into your memories, both of you should stand, preferably barefoot, and take a few deep breaths. Feel yourself standing still and strong, your feet firm on the ground, as if you were growing your own roots into the earth. You will feel at peace and empowered, and also connected with your sibling, who will be doing the same. This will place you both in a calm and curious mindset.

— Memory Sharing: Take turns sharing your childhood memories. You need to start with the root memories, your original core stories, which undergird how you learned what was acceptable between you two and what was not. You will have to breathe through this to control your fight-flight-freeze mechanisms. (We'll get into the nitty-gritty of Memory Sharing in Chapter 8).

— Celebrate yourselves: End each session by praising yourself and each other for powering through.

— Record sessions: You should both record your meetings so that nothing gets forgotten.

Participants:

This work is between just the two of you for the first four weeks. This is another way to protect the process. Your parents and other siblings add layers of complexity to your dynamic, and at this point, the two of you need a little space to get your footing without their interference. This will give you time to acknowledge how your family members participated in your sibling conflict. Don't worry, there will be a right time to share your work with them, and we will offer suggestions on how to do this. **<u>See Chapter 10 for a deeper description of why this plays a crucial and necessary role in the process</u>**.

Short-Term Goals:

- Show up to every call.

- Decide together how to reschedule. For example, you can agree not to wait until the last minute when you realize something has come up, and instead you commit to communicating the moment you become aware there's a conflict in your schedule.

- Notice your common triggers during your calls and during your day-to-day as well.

We suggest you each keep a printed copy of the contract and read it over as often as necessary to keep the flow fresh in your mind and carry the Prime Directive in your heart. Since this is your own unique sibling contract, we want you to add or change whatever makes sense to you. Your short-term goals are your own. If you want to incorporate meditation or some other ritual, we love that, too. What we've provided you is a basic building block. Sign it, stamp it, or don't, but make sure it's present as you get into the next steps of the process.

CHAPTER 7

Step 2 – Identify Your Archetypes

Now that you have begun to create how you would like your new sibling culture to be, it's time to dismantle the old one. To do that, you and your sibling must free yourselves of the archetypes that defined your relationship under your old sibling culture.

You might be familiar with the term "archetype" in relation to the fairy tales you read as a kid. In these stories, archetypes are universally recognized character types who fulfill a specific role to advance the plot. You know them as the hero or heroine, the evil stepmother, the sidekick, the fairy godmother. They have a broad set of characteristics and generally fall into one of two camps: good or evil, helpful or unhelpful. Archetypes are not interested in nuance or complexity. They're two-dimensional. And crucially, archetypes can't exist on their own. They work in relation to each other. A hero can only be a hero if he has a villain to fight, just as a fairy godmother can only be a fairy godmother if she has a hero to guide.

How does this apply to you and your sibling? Well obviously, human beings are much more complex than 2-D character types. But because we are storytellers who make sense of the world by creating narratives, we often, whether unconsciously or not, categorize the people we know into archetypes, or roles we believe they fulfill. And one of the first places we do this is in our families. As their children's creators - or authors - parents are often the ones who first ascribe archetypes to their kids.

> *Deep Dive*: Dr. Carl Jung developed the idea of archetypes as part of the collective unconscious–the universal ideas and thoughts across cultures, in myths, fairytales and dreams. There are Caregiver, Ruler, Artist, Innocent, Sage, Explorer, Outlaw, Magician, Hero, Lover, Jester and Everyman.

In our case, our mom, our main caretaker, was the primary author of the archetypes we ended up embodying. She wasn't conscious of it, but here's how it happened.

To our mom, Jessica was the problem child - the one she struggled to control; the one with whom she spent excruciating hours pouring over textbooks to help her with her homework because of Jessica's dyslexia. On the other hand, Bluma was the easy child - the one she easily connected with emotionally; the one she didn't have to worry about in school. As we explained in Chapter 3, there are several complicated reasons why our mom felt this way, many having to do with her relationship with her own mother, and her attempts to make sure the second-born daughter wasn't less favored the way she had been. The point is, even though our mom insisted she loved us both equally, it felt as if she preferred Bluma over Jessica. We both saw and felt it.

Even though we never put a label to it, growing up we felt as if we embodied two roles. Bluma was the Favorite, and Jessica was the Black Sheep. If "the Favorite" and "the Black Sheep" sound like characters out of a children's book, that's no coincidence. Roles, or archetypes, are largely fictional. We weren't actually the Favorite or the Black Sheep, we were just playing those parts, just like you might play the hero or the evil stepmother in a school play. And just like a hero and an evil stepmother, the Favorite and the Black Sheep are two-dimensional, and can only exist in relation to each other. You can't have a Favorite without a Black Sheep, since one role only exists when compared to the other.

Our archetypes defined our dynamic. Like actors in a play, we felt like we'd been handed a script and instructed to act and react to each other based on those parts. Our mom - call her the director in this metaphor - had assigned us these roles. But the more we played them, the more difficult it became for us to separate ourselves from these parts. We became method actors, unable to shed our characters to become our true selves.

Our roles seeped into our relationships with our other family members. Bluma was the Favorite in relation to our mom, in part because of her natural ability to read people and to simplify their emotions to them. She was so good at it, in fact, that our parents turned to her as a sort of therapist, asking her to arbitrate their marital disputes. In time, Bluma also brought these skills to her relationships with our younger siblings, especially following our parents' divorce. Jessica was off building her married life, our brother Adam was in rabbinical school, and the rest of our family - our mom, our younger sister Sara, and Bluma - moved into a small apartment. It was a turbulent time: our dad often neglected to pay child support, and we struggled to adjust from having lived in a large, comfortable house to suddenly being cramped in an apartment that was, frankly, less nice than a college dorm. Our younger sister, a freshman in high school, and our mom clashed constantly, and our mom's patience wore thin. Bluma took it upon herself to be a source of order and comfort: she acted as a second mother to our younger sister, and a source of support to our mom.

As for Jessica, the feelings of rejection and of being misunderstood by our mom also crept into her relationships with our other family members. She felt excluded from the tight-knit circle that Bluma, our mom and our younger sister formed. She often felt like it was them against her, a belief that was reinforced by our mom's repeated avowals that Jessica "always made it worse" whenever there was some kind of argument among any of us. Jessica was made to feel like everything was her fault. She was the outlier.

It's simple. The more you're told you are something, the more times you experience it, the more you start believing it, and behaving like it. And this had both negative and positive consequences for both of us.

On the surface, it may seem like the Favorite was the more enviable position and the Black Sheep, the more painful role. But that's not true either. For Bluma, her whole history with our family consisted of listening and problem-solving. She invested a ton of energy and time into making sure the family was OK. Who was checking to make sure Bluma's needs were met? Well, often, it felt like no one. The Favorite could be a lonely and miserable place to be, too. Meanwhile, despite all the pain that Jessica's position as the Black Sheep gave her, it also became a source of strength. Since no one was going to fight for her, she learned to do it on her own. Her role as the Black Sheep endowed Jessica with an independent spirit and a drive to work towards her goals, no matter what or who stood in the way.

Over time, we identified with those roles so much that they even defined us beyond our home. Bluma acted as a therapist to her friends, attending to their emotional needs, even if it meant sacrificing her own happiness for their sake. Among her friends, Jessica prioritized her own needs, since no one at home did, which occasionally ended up alienating her from them.

Our archetypes were useful in some ways, but hurting us in many others. And crucially, our archetypes had frozen us in the past. There was no way we could be better sisters - and happier people - as long as we played the roles we'd been forced to play since we were children.

That's why Step 2 of the healing process is defining your archetype. You can only free yourself from your role by naming it.

Because here's the thing. You are **not** your archetype. It's just a category, a broad stroke, and you are so much more than that. You may embody some of your archetype's characteristics, but probably not all of them. And - this is the most important takeaway - you weren't born this way. You were assigned your role, probably by your primary caregiver, and then kept performing it, either out of habit, or in an effort to win their affection/attention. As we've explained, our earliest development hinges on our desire to feel more accepted, and less rejected, by our parents. And performing the archetypes we're assigned is one of the primary ways we do this.

For you and your sibling to see each other as you truly are - off stage and out of costume - it's crucially important to define your archetypes for the following three reasons.

First, by naming it, you give yourself validation. Even if you weren't consciously aware you were playing a role, you could see how your family reacted to you and your sibling differently. As the Black Sheep, for example, Jessica often felt excluded. And as the Favorite, Bluma felt stuck in the role of being everyone's caretaker. By recognizing our roles, we could finally admit to ourselves that these feelings were not in our heads. If your parents have always insisted that you and your siblings were loved and treated just the same, but you know deep down that this simply did not feel true, well then, recognizing your archetypes with your sibling will finally put an end to the misbelief.

Second, naming your archetype makes it lose its power. If you've ever gone to therapy and spoken about a traumatic memory for the first time ever, you'll know what we're talking about. When we repress painful thoughts, they take on a life of their own. They become bigger and scarier, which makes us want to repress them even more. The act of saying them out loud strips them of their power over us. They're no longer unspeakable and unnameable. You now have power over them, since you can wield your words and form them into the narrative you want. The same is true for your archetype. By calling it out, you empower yourself.

And finally, by defining your archetype, you separate yourself from it. You can look at it as a discrete, digestible piece of information, and you can choose to view it with curiosity and compassion. It's a way to make it feel less loaded. Here's another way of putting it. If Bluma says, "Jessica was difficult growing up," that's a value judgment on Jessica that will hurt her. It attacks her very essence. If, however, Bluma says, "Jessica was the Black Sheep," there's an understanding that Bluma is referring to the role Jessica was made to play. It's not who she was at her core, but how she acted in response to her environment. And that allows both of us to look at the Black Sheep role as something we can analyze and pick apart. Jessica can decide that she likes some characteristics of the Black Sheep and hold on to them - like her independence and originality - and she can choose to discard the parts of the Black Sheep that don't serve her. You can do the same. You can pick and choose what you want to hang on to and what you're now free to leave behind.

It was freeing and liberating to finally voice and define our archetypes. Those roles explained so much about our dynamic, and why we felt like we were in competition with each other. It had been set up that way. Once you figure out your own archetypes, you'll feel renewed, too.

So now you're probably wondering, how do you get there?

For us, it was shockingly quick and easy. It came up in one of our very first Zoom conversations. Bluma was the one who brought it up first. It was a difficult thing to admit, but since we were being honest, she felt like she had to share it. She told Jessica that growing up, she could see how our mom related differently to her. The way she engaged with Jessica almost looked like the way a person would interact with a step-child. There was something a bit awkward and distant about it. For Bluma, it was incredibly uncomfortable to witness, but it also made her feel relieved and grateful our mom didn't treat her that way.

This was hard for Jessica to hear, not because it was news to her. It was painful because it was the truth.

It was a revelation we somehow already knew deep in our bones. So we said it. Bluma was the Favorite, and Jessica was the Black Sheep. It was that simple.

It may not be that easy for you, and that's completely fine. Defining your archetype may be a process that takes a few weeks as you work on the next step of the healing process. You might change your mind about which archetype resonates with you, or realize that you've played different ones during different phases of your life. We settled on the Favorite and the Black Sheep, but there are countless others. You and your sibling could have been the Influencer and the Influenced. One sibling may have been the older, cool high schooler, for example, which the younger sibling looked up to and hoped to emulate. Maybe you were the Worshiped and the Irrelevant. One sibling could have attracted a lot of attention and praise, while the other sibling felt invisible in their shadow. Or you could have been the Peacemaker and the Instigator. You get the idea. We want you to choose the archetypes that feel right to you. Just remember, they are roles that exist in opposition to each other, or at the expense of another. We want you to be as creative as you want. Take your time figuring it out, and just make sure the two of you are on the same page. Also, we want to stress the fact that it's important you not worry about what you think other people may think of your archetype. If you felt like you were made to play a particular role, that's what it was. It's about your experience. You don't need to worry about whether you think your parents, other siblings, or friends would agree with you. In fact, very often parents don't corroborate their adult child's version of events.

It's not about accuracy, it's about authenticity

To settle on your archetypes, you'll have to dig deep and talk it out together. To help you out, we've outlined a few questions to guide you as you reflect.

In your family

What was your relationship with your sibling?

___

___

___

What was your relationship with your caregiver?

___

What did you do with your caregiver regularly? (These can include activities like grocery shopping, going to synagogue/church, going out to eat at certain places, watching a series, reading books etc.)

___

What was your "thing" together, if you had one?

___

What does your sibling recognize as a thing you did with your parents that was exclusive to just you?

___

What things did you feel excluded from?

_____

_____

_____

What do you feel like you were each encouraged or discouraged to do to fulfill these roles?

_____

_____

_____

In your friendships, relationships, and at work

What role do you feel you take on in these environments?

_____

_____

_____

How do you feel about being seen as that person in your friend group, work environment, etc? Do you like it and seek that out, or do you resent it and feel stuck in that role?

_____

_____

_____

When was the last time you remember seeking to surround yourself with people who reinforce these roles?

_____

_____

_____

Your archetypes will provide a framework for accessing your feelings and memories from the past in Step 3 of the healing process. Again, don't worry if you haven't totally figured it out yet as you move into the next step; you can work on these steps simultaneously.

CHAPTER 8

Step 3 - Memory Sharing

This, we think, is the most exciting part of the process. You're going to feel a lot of feelings, and you're going to learn so much about yourself, your sibling, and your dynamic. You're Indiana Jones, excavating your memories. You might find some mummies along the way, but you'll be having an adventure, surrounded by a trusted team of archeologists. That's your sibling, and us. And at the end of the line, you won't believe the treasure you find.

It's time to dive into the past with Step 3 - Memory Sharing.

Before we get into the Memory Sharing process, we want to explain how we decided it was vital we do this.

Realizing that we'd both abused each other growing up felt like a giant step forward. *After years - decades, in fact - we were both finally on the same page, both aware that we'd played equally important parts in each other's suffering.* We understood that in the sibling abuse we inflicted on each other, there was no <u>one</u> victim, and there was no <u>one</u> aggressor. It was a powerful realization for each of us, and on that phone call, back in late 2019, it was the first, decisive step in the direction of uniting as siblings. That was clear. What was less clear was *how* we should move forward from there.

We did have one clue. We'd both sensed some version of the same message, "She is where you need to go"; that phrase that had struck Bluma while she was in the shower and that prompted her to video call Jessica. It was a strange instruction. It sounded literal, but we knew, deep down, that we weren't meant to hop on a plane to see each other. The fact that a global pandemic broke out mere weeks later, grounding us in countries halfway around the world from each other, made that impossible anyway. This place - where we, as siblings, each were - was not geographic. *It was a place lost in time.* We had to time travel to find each other as kids, as young people forming our views on the world, and of each other.

To repair our broken relationship, we had to get to know each other all over again to understand - with curiosity and compassion - why the girls we had once been had grown into the women we now were: adults who felt triggered at the mere sight of each other, even hearing each other's name. We had to understand the core, original story of our relationship.

Picture your sibling relationship like a tree. Most of what you see is above ground: one trunk reaching towards the sky, dozens of branches springing out of it in all directions, and hundreds of leaves growing out of them. All of these different parts are manifestations and reflections of your sibling relationship. The branches and leaves represent all of the experiences you've shared. They all emanate from a single trunk, and deeper than that, from roots deep in the ground. They're the essence of your relationship that colors and shapes every experience you have - all the branches and leaves. Day to day, you may not even be conscious of those roots, because they're buried so deep. But those roots are your core, original stories.

And, the core of your sibling relationship wants to be healed. The Zeigarnik Effect is in full swing: both of your minds are desperately trying to resolve all the conflict from your childhood that has gone unfixed and unprocessed all these years. This part of you, the part of you that is a sibling, wants you to pay attention to it, and it will keep making noise until you do.

Let's move away from our tree metaphor for a moment and put it this way. We're all made of different parts. You, as an individual, might be a teacher, a mother, a sister, a friend, a runner, a reader, an adventure seeker, and a myriad of other things that make you who you are. Occasionally, these different facets might feel at odds with each other. Think about it. Haven't you ever thought or said, "Part of me feels really excited about this, but part of me is anxious"? Or "Part of me is bored with the plan, but part of me feels excited about it"? That's because all of our different life experiences and relationships combine to inform our views in different ways. One part of you could crave adventure because as a kid, your parents took you sailing and camping and you learned to love it. Or because your parents were terrified of everything and never let you spread your wings, so now you can't get enough. Another part of you could be nervous about heights because one time you got stuck on a roller coaster mid-plunge. So now, when your friend suggests you join them to hike a peak, part of you may jump at the opportunity - the adventurer - while another part of you may worry about the danger involving heights. That's entirely normal. However, what if the adventurer, out of a need to fill the craving for danger, took excessive risks with negative consequences, even though the quieter, more cautious part of him wished he wouldn't. This interplay is an illustration of what psychologist Dr. Richard Schwartz discovered in his theory on Internal Family Systems, which holds that our internal world is made up of different parts.

Bluma often says she has two speeds: glam or hobo. In glam-mode she feels sexy, confident, put-together and important, while in hobo-mode, she feels comfortable, carefree and laid back. Both are parts of her personality that make up who she is. But some days they're in conflict with each other. For example, if Bluma expects to show up to an important interview or meeting in glam-mode but wakes up late and has to hobo it, her confidence might take a hit. It's not easy, but it is very important to be curious in these moments; to see what Glam-Bluma is feeling, find a way to adjust and pivot so it doesn't take over and interfere with the outcome she hoped for in the interview or meeting. Because Glam-Bluma or Hobo-Bluma are only sub-parts of her, and she can access her strengths regardless of what she wears or how she feels. Being integrated means that she knows that Glam-Bluma and Hobo-Bluma are passengers in her car, but she is the one driving.

When we struggle to integrate - when we cannot assimilate certain experiences into our sense of self, we can really suffer in the long term. This is called dissociation or compartmentalization. It's a protective mechanism at first; a way for your mind to shut out painful experiences because they feel overwhelming in the moment. But as much as you try to keep the experiences out of sight and out of mind, they are still happening - they're still lurking somewhere in your subconscious - and they will fight to be seen and heard.

This is common for trauma survivors. Many initially block out a painful memory to continue on with their lives as if nothing had happened. But in time, this becomes more and more impossible. The painful memory butts up against all other experiences and discolors their lives. Trauma survivors will often experience depression, anxiety, and even an increased risk for infection and disease because of the continuous stress they experience. They may also unconsciously reenact versions of the same original trauma. A person who was mugged and never processed the attack may unwittingly find themselves becoming avoidant of everyday situations, or putting themselves in dangerous situations where they face a risk of harm (think Batman or Spiderman). This is a subconscious attempt to resolve the first traumatic experience. Ultimately, the way to move forward is to move *through* the original trauma (the one being avoided). Processing it consciously, helps integrate it into your story, as a *part* of what makes you, you. And that is the beginning of healing yourself.

We all have unprocessed trauma from our earliest childhood experiences with our sibling. That's no one's fault, and you're not alone. You were both kids. Kids aren't born with a rulebook, and your brain isn't developed to reflect on experiences in that way, at that stage. Your primary caregiver is meant to help you navigate the nuances of being a human in society. And our society does not encourage us as adults to get therapy for hostile sibling relationships. There is a part of you - the part that feels a deep sense of hurt from your sibling, a pain that started long ago, when you were a child - that is desperately trying to climb out of your subconscious. It wants to be seen and heard. It wants to be integrated.

And until it is, it will make as much noise as possible to get you to pay attention.

In our case, the parts of us that were in pain from our sibling dynamic had very loud voices and could easily dominate us. For Bluma, for example, feeling a sense of injustice was a huge trigger. Against her better judgment, if she felt like someone didn't understand her and spoke or acted in a way that was unjust, she would tell that person exactly what she thought and how she felt. It didn't matter if that person was a professor or a boss. It felt out of her control because it often sabotaged her in some way. Now she knows that what was going on was that the part of her that, for so long, had felt unjustly attacked by Jessica and had been powerless to fight back, was clamoring to stand up for herself, even if it meant a 'slap' in the face.

For Jessica, feeling like she wasn't seen was a trigger. From the time she was a kid, she'd always made sure to make her presence known. She was loud and needed the limelight. When it was her birthday, she'd proclaim it before anyone had a chance to wish her a happy day. Just like Bluma, this was also an unconscious act of self sabotage. Because the idea of someone forgetting her birthday, of not seeing her, was so painful to Jessica, she made sure no one had a chance to forget. By jumping the gun and announcing it herself, she was robbing herself of the pleasure of being surprised, of being cared for without demanding recognition or affection. Now she knows that the part of her that, for so long, had felt overshadowed by Bluma in front of our mom, had felt like she had to compete with Bluma for our mom's affection, was shouting to be seen and cared for.

These parts of us were not helping us thrive as adults, but we couldn't stop them. They were too powerful. In order to wrestle control back from them, we had to stop and listen to them. We had to ask ourselves, and eventually each other, "What do you need?"

Because we carried the answers within us, and in each other. Those answers lay in our core, original stories, which were lodged in these parts of us that had not yet been processed together.

So this is why we go back to the beginning. This is why sharing your memories of your "loudest" sibling relationship pain points is so vital to the process.

Now you may be wondering, just how exactly do you choose which core original stories - which pain points - to share? It's actually remarkably simple. Close your eyes and ask yourself,

"What are the memories from my childhood about my sibling relationship that still make me mad or sad?"

It's important you think back to your childhood and not remember events from your more recent adult lives. When you think of examples of things your sibling has done that make you mad or sad, a bunch of slights, insults or fights, as fresh as the one you saw, heard or actively participated in a week, a month, or a year ago, might come up for you. But those aren't your core stories. Going back to our tree metaphor, those are your branches and leaves. They're what's grown out of the seed. To find the heart of the tree, you have to dig deeper in time, into your roots - your childhood - to find the first or most important experiences that shaped your understanding of your sibling.

That's why we suggest you think of five or less childhood core memories. Beyond that, they're just outgrowths of the same core stories, just more leaves and branches.

So to start Step 3 of the healing process, we want each of you to **select up to five core memories**.

— We suggest you start out by each, individually, brain-dumping a list of all the memories, events and triggers that come up for you as the biggest pain points (as you memory share, you'll begin to see how some of the memories that didn't make the "top 5" are outgrowths of the core original pain points; if not, you'll practice the skills of Memory Sharing with the "top 5" and can circle back to one of the other memories to create healing there too).

— Then, whittle this list down to no more than five items of the memories that elicit the strongest emotions. The list can contain fewer than five; just no more than that.

— Next, share your lists with each other in writing. You can email or text or mail them; it doesn't matter. Just

STEP 3 – MEMORY SHARING

make sure your sibling can read your list, and you can read theirs, prior to your first Memory Sharing. This will allow each of you to take it in at your own pace. Because, some memories may be obvious; some may be a surprise; but all will likely elicit feelings. Giving each other a chance to let that first wave or emotion pass allows each of you the space and grace to breathe through and begin with eyes wide open.

We'll share examples of our own core memories to give you an idea of what worked for us. For Bluma, it was a memory of Jessica chasing her. She was four and Jessica was seven. Jessica was mad and running after her, and Bluma managed to sprint inside our bedroom, shut the door, and pin her back against it to stop Jessica from forcing it open. She remembers, in meticulous detail, the sensation of Jessica - her stronger, older sister - pushing against the wooden door. As she pushed back, Bluma stared at a set of cardboard drawers stacked in a corner. When she thinks about the memory now, she can still smell the cardboard. But more than anything, she remembers the absolute terror she felt, the thought that Jessica was going to actually kill her. She believed she would always feel like this, that she would always have to run away from Jessica, that Jessica could destroy her.

It's a powerful memory Bluma immediately knew she had to share. It made sense that it would be the first on her list.

For Jessica, it was a memory of our mom driving us to tap dance class in the VW rabbit, around the same ages as we were in Bluma's memory, seven and four. We were sitting in the backseat, rolling past cotton fields, and we were bickering nonstop. Bluma kept saying mean things to Jessica, and Jessica kept asking our mom to tell Bluma to stop. Our mom didn't answer her or intervene, and Bluma kept on saying mean things. So Jessica snapped and hit Bluma hard and kept on hitting. Jessica had gotten the message that unless she took some kind of action herself, no one was going to do it for her. What happened, however, is that Bluma started crying, and our mom pulled the car over to yank Jessica off her sister, telling her she couldn't behave that way. Jessica was the only one who was punished when she had not even started the fight. It was deeply unfair, and it was a blueprint for how her future interactions with Bluma would unfold.

Jessica wrote it down on her list.

After you've shared your list of memories with each other, but before you meet to discuss them, we'd like you to think about your hopes, hesitations and expectations regarding the Memory Sharing exercise. To help you with this process, we've created a Pre-Memory-Sharing questionnaire. This is a tool for you to concretize what has historically only ever been in your head. Remember to use other tools we shared in Chapter 5, such as breathing and grounding, to help keep you centered as you unearth the memories on your Memory Sharing list, with all the feelings, fears/hopes and bodily sensations that are associated with them. These will arise, and the tools above will help you stay present and more relaxed as you are downloading your list. Write your answers down. The writing process helps to crystallize your thoughts. If you're not a writer, no problem:
- Use a dictation app that transcribes your thoughts. Although your 5 core memories are for sharing, you get to decide how

much of the feelings, hopes and fears you want to include. It may feel too vulnerable at first, so take the pace that feels right to you.

Pre-Memory Sharing

Here are the questions:

Describe, in a few sentences, your memory. (e.g. "I was around 6 years old. We were fishing in Ruidoso, New Mexico, and we fought over the top-bunk in our cabin. You threatened me, I kicked you and we broke the bed. We were grounded and had to work all summer with no music and no friends.")

_____

_____

_____

_____

_____

_____

Share the feelings around this memory. (e.g. "I worried it would never end; I felt like I was helpless.")

_____

_____

_____

_____

_____

_____

What need(s) are related to this memory? (e.g. "The need to be in control; the need to feel safe.")

_____

_____

_____

_____

_____

_____

How is this need being served within us today? (e.g. "Striving always to be on time or being first or winning; being a peacemaker; avoiding conflict")

_____

_____

_____

_____

_____

Once you've answered these questions, we'd like you to think about what you expect or hope will come out of sharing these memories with your sibling. Here are a few more questions you can answer in writing:

What do you worry will happen when you share this memory?

_____

_____

_____

_____

_____

What do you hope to hear from your sibling after you share this memory?

_____

_____

_____

_____

_____

What do you hope to feel following this memory share?

_____

_____

_____

_____

_____

And now, when you're ready, we'd like you to begin to traverse these memories together. Yes, it is a journey you're taking *together*, going back in time, but this time you have the added bonus of having an adult perspective.

When you meet each other on Zoom - after you've taken time to Shoot The Shit and to Ground yourselves - you should decide who shares first, and how. Whoever begins should then choose one of their memories and talk about it in whatever way makes sense to them. That could involve describing the sensory details they remember (like sweaty palms, shallow breathing, fight-or-flight reactions), or the feelings it elicits, or how it fits into a bigger pattern of conflict in your relationship. If you are struggling to find feelings, refer to the list we have provided in the feeling list in Chapter 2 and the Continuums in Chapters 3, 4 and 11.

The Prime Directive is your guide in creating your new sibling dynamic. You want to share authentically, with the goal of being understood. It is not an attempt to convince your sibling and "finally be right". That will only lead to more of the same default pattern you and your sibling have struggled with all these years, just like Jessica and Bluma did. Once you've shared your experience, the other sibling will have the opportunity to respond.

This is not meant to be a rigid or strict formula. The structure we've created helps keep you on a new path to not fall back to default patterns. We encourage you to let it flow as naturally as it can. To do that, you'll want to pay close attention to what you're feeling, and what you're picking up from your sibling. If you notice your chest tighten or your hands shake when you share your memory, share this sensation with your sibling. If you notice your sibling tense up as you speak, take a beat from sharing the memory and ask them what's happening. Let them explain why they're feeling triggered. As your sibling is talking, do other memories come up? Does it make sense to share it, or return to the original memory you started out with?

There is no wrong answer. Your reactions to the memories are what's most important here. You have to follow the triggers. They hold the answers.

As you share your memories, you should feel free to communicate what you understand to be your sibling's part in the memory. You may both feel some resistance to being cast as the bad guy in your sibling's memory, and may remember things differently. That's OK. The goal is not to get your sibling to agree 100% with you, but to allow them to see the memory from your perspective and empathize. This will allow them to acknowledge your version of events, and accept their role in your pain, without compromising their own reality.

We encourage you to forgive each other, and accept each other's forgiveness.

It's vital to keep the Prime Directive in mind. While listening to your sibling describe how you contributed to the pain they felt, stay curious and compassionate. Curiosity will allow you to see the memory as an interesting story you want to understand, not as an accusation you need to defend yourself against. Compassion will keep your heart open and help your sibling release the burden of their pain. This might sound like a tough thing to do right now. Since you have your own perspective on your shared childhood, you might not see eye to eye. That's fine. You can still take ownership and accept the part you played in your sibling's memory. This isn't betraying your version of the truth, or punishing yourself. It's acknowledging your sibling's understanding of events. We like to say, it's an acknowledge-y, not an apology. An acknowledge-y allows you to honor and validate what someone else feels in a way that allows them to feel heard and understood (e.g. "That makes sense that you would feel scared of me when I chased you as kids" or "That is frustrating and unfair that mom made you feel solely at fault so much of the time"). And remember, you will get your turn to speak. When you do, your sibling will also be working on staying curious and compassionate about your version of events.

The Memory Sharing process is a dance between the two of you. It's a waltz, a tango, a salsa - whatever partnered dance you'd like to imagine. There are a series of steps you should be repeating, but the order in which you do them - when you choose to spin or twirl or pause - that's a matter of improvisation. You're in charge of the choreography. You're responding to each other's bodies, to your triggers, to your reactions.

When sharing and listening, the following tips will help you to stay on track, and will help you keep the Prime Directive alive.

Sharing Tips:

— Focus on your own experience. Try not to get distracted by your assumptions of how your sibling is feeling or thinking, unless that's a part of your story. Yet, if it happens, jot it down so you can come back to it.

— Remember that the goal in sharing is to elicit compassion, remorse and understanding from your sibling. Just as you want them to understand they were responsible for making you feel a certain way and to own that responsibility, you too must work to forgive them when they do.

— Don't worry about remembering every minute detail—this isn't about accuracy, it's about sharing your authentic feelings attached to YOUR memory.

Listening Tips:

— Try not to focus on correcting details of the memory—this isn't about accuracy, it's about authenticity.

— If something comes up for you that you think is important to discuss, jot it down so that you don't interrupt your sibling's flow. If you need to, ask your sibling to pause so you can take a note.

— Be remorseful. Even if you don't remember the memory your sibling is sharing, or you remember it differently, realize that what they're sharing is a burden they've been carrying since childhood.

— Take ownership from a place of compassion.

As sisters, we had many shared experiences. But the ways we remembered them were often completely different - from the granular details to the relative importance we assigned them in our minds. Bluma tends to remember minute details, while Jessica is more focused on the feelings she remembers experiencing. We both had to accept that neither of us was wrong in our recollections. You can't have a healing conversation about a memory if you keep telling each other their memories are wrong. Memory Sharing is not the time to squabble over details. If your sibling insists something happened in the third grade, but you're convinced it was the fourth grade, let it go, for now.

There's a reason you might want to hold on to details like times and dates. Perfectionism is a coping mechanism, and it is often related to repeated exposure to trauma. When we feel our actions are constantly being monitored, scrutinized and retaliated against, we try to control whatever we can. Fears of inadequacy, worthlessness, failure and loss are often at the root of this drive. Focusing around "accuracy" may make you feel like you're in control, but it's actually letting fear frame the process. Instead, we urge you to allow trust to be the frame of this step of the process. Because you'll only hurt each other more by invalidating each other's lived experiences when focusing on micro details.

We'll say it again: *This is not about accuracy. It's about authenticity.*

After each Memory Share, we recommend you take some time to reflect. We've created a Post-Memory-Sharing survey to help you. Take a minute to answer the following questions.

POST-Game Memory Share Survey

Was there anything you heard that was different from what you had remembered?

_____

_____

_____

_____

How does knowing others' memory-shares shape how you feel about your memory, if at all?

_____

_____

_____

_____

_____

STEP 3 - MEMORY SHARING

What are you feeling now, physically, emotionally, mentally?

_____

_____

_____

_____

_____

_____

How was it to share this memory with _____?
How did _____ receive your memory?

_____

_____

_____

_____

_____

_____

Are any need(s) related to this memory still left unresolved? Were there any expectations unfulfilled or a part of the memory you both didn't "go there"?

_____

_____

_____

_____

_____

How do you imagine things will be different when the issues from this memory get triggered (cuz they will)? Consider typical scenarios and generate re-formed responses.

_____

_____

_____

_____

_____

As we said at the beginning, Memory Sharing is like an archeological excavation into your past. You'll be digging deep, and pulling some heavy artifacts to the surface. It will feel different, yet challenging. So be kind to each other, and to yourself. Make sure you self-care. In the next chapter, we're going to guide you on how to manage your emotions while you walk down memory lane. We're with you every step of the way. You're doing great, and we're so proud of you.

CHAPTER 9

Step 4 - Learning To Move Through Conflict

As you share your memories and acknowledge the parts you both played in each other's pain, you will probably feel some old, familiar feelings bubbling to the surface. You may feel irritated. You may feel misunderstood. You may feel hurt. You may feel numb or confused. Multiple emotions are completely normal: you're unearthing difficult past experiences that are, in a way, having you time travel to those very moments and reminding you of how you felt then. You are getting triggered.

This may sound unpleasant. But here's the thing - leaning *into* the triggers is what will ultimately set you free. Getting curious about them and exploring the reasons why you get upset, frustrated or sad during your Zoom sessions will help you understand why your childhood relationship veered off a path of love and support and grew into one of resentment and contempt. It's like restoring an old house. You can't just slap on a coat of paint: you may have to patch up the walls, or overturn some old stones and lay down some new ones, or even build an entirely new foundation. At the end of the process, you'll have a beautiful, sturdy house together.

What you don't want to do is concuss your head or end up with an arm in a cast. That would not only delay the house-building process, but leave you in pain and out of commission. Likewise, navigating the triggers and hurt, and the upset they may bring, should be a constructive pursuit - not a destructive one. That's why Step 4 of our process is learning to move through conflict. When friction or misunderstanding between you and your sibling occurs, having a competence to have practical and positive dialogue allows healing to continue, instead of detracting from it.

Conflict and connection are at the heart of the human experience. As social beings, all of our thoughts, needs, desires, values and interests intersect with other people, and don't always line up nice and neat. Therefore, it's important to know ways to treat others with respect and dignity while also honoring how *you* feel. This balance is something you start reckoning with at a very young age. Imagine an older brother assembles his Thomas and Friends trains and his younger brother messes it up. Conflict. Or a younger sister cuts her older sister's Barbie's hair. Conflict. Or a pair of siblings compete over who gets to call "shotgun" first. Conflict. When these points of tension occur, typically a fight breaks out, one person feels right and thinks their sibling is stupid, and we stay stuck in these childhood patterns. That is an opportunity lost for true connection, because conflict provides opportunities for siblings to both emotionally regulate (Chapter 5) and process the issue

STEP 4 - LEARNING TO MOVE THROUGH CONFLICT

so they resolve it and build a deeper mutual understanding. Connection.

As adults, we knew full well we did not have a good sibling relationship, and our conflicts made us spiral out with each other. Like we've said, we weren't taught to process conflict productively. What we knew was rage - vomit our anger out with our words and our actions, and get it out of our systems as fast as possible. So we did that, but we never felt better after the upheaval, and it never resolved the conflict. Negative feelings would hover over and around us, like an *emotional hangover.*

The memories of our childhood relationship felt like a black hole sucking us in every time we thought about each other, a pull force into darkness that we couldn't escape. Once we each realized we had to mend our relationship in order to escape that negative force, it was obvious to each of us that we had to build a new, functional and stable space in which we could calmly and constructively address conflict.

1. How does your sibling relationship keep holding you both in historical, unhelpful patterns? What patterns do you feel controlled by, which, even though you want to change, seem like you can't?

_____

_____

_____

_____

2. What patterns does your sibling seem controlled by too?

_____

_____

_____

_____

3. What other scenarios can you recall more recently that you wished you had shown up differently?

_____

_____

_____

_____

4. Where have you had these conflicts with other people?

_____

_____

_____

_____

STEP 4 - LEARNING TO MOVE THROUGH CONFLICT

5. How are these patterns similar to your sibling conflict? Different? .

___

___

___

___

We wondered: How could we train ourselves to handle friction and disputes together when no one had ever taught us how? We decided we had to look back - way back - and see what a healthy relationship looked like for young kids. As you grow up, you learn coping mechanisms to help you move through the world in a way that shields you from pain. This is a healthy endeavor: self-preservation is key to survival. As we described in Chapter 2, the early experiences you had assessing risk and safety primed you to cope with conflict in similar ways. You may instinctively prioritize defending yourself rather than staying open and curious about why someone might be confronting you. However, when you're a small child, you're still developing your understanding of the world. Those coping mechanisms have started forming, yet they're not cemented yet. That's why we wanted to look at the ways siblings in elementary school confront conflict.

Think of a playground; the ordered chaos that is children at play. Some are running and playing tag, others are teamed up playing soccer or crouched down exchanging Pokèmon cards, others are jumping rope or playing hopscotch, some are twisting themselves onto, pulling up or flying off monkey bars and others still are playing hide-and-seek. It's a landscape full of joy, delight and imagination, but one that is also primed for strife. Some games will butt up into others. There may not be enough soccer balls to go around. One kid may be hogging the monkey bars. Another may want to join the hopscotch crew, but the hoppers have decided they already have too many people playing, so reject the newcomer.

Now imagine a landscape populated by siblings, where parents are meant to mitigate these conflicts. There are so many complex relationships at play, and each of these relationships carries its own complex history. There's the sibling history, the child-parent history, and for the parents, their own sibling and parental histories, which color their understanding of their children's dynamic and their role as parents. On top of that, parents often feel their children's behavior reflects on them, and they may react disproportionately out of fear or concern of how others will judge them. All these factors blend together, forming the patterns of behavior and communication amongst siblings and the parent-child relationship. And if a pattern gets set, everyone involved learns to expect it. This pattern conditions everyone's behavior and reaction. This becomes a game of family twister.

1. Can you see common family dynamics related to your parents' history with their siblings?

---

2. What kind of relationship do your parents have with their siblings now?

3. Looking at your parents' relationship with their sibling, can you see similarities in your sibling relationship?

Dr. Laurie Kramer is a psychologist who has extensively researched how to help young siblings get along with each other in her program, More Fun with Brothers and Sisters. She teaches young siblings the skills they need to help them build positive, long-lasting relationships. One of the foundational tenets this program teaches is how to accept or decline an invitation to play - basically, how to treat others with respect and dignity while also honoring how you feel. It's so simple, but so important. It teaches them how to say, "I want to play with you" or "I don't want to play with you" in a way that clearly communicates intent without leading to hurt feelings or any other damage. This simple frame is foundational because it applies to situations and relationships we have throughout our lives.

Kids are unfiltered. It's what makes them delightful, pure, and also occasionally difficult. A child who doesn't get their way will say exactly how they feel. Imagine 5-year-old Sam asks his friend Darren to play tag with him at recess, but Darren does not want to and says no. Sam, who is hurt (rejected) because Darren does not want to be his buddy at that moment, shouts, "You're stupid and I hate you!" and kicks Darren's leg as Sam walks away. And Darren, who is hurt by Sam's comment and kick, yells back, "I hate you more!" Now they're fighting.

An adult witnessing this fight could step in to help them learn how to honor what they want, set a boundary, and still remain friends. Darren is entitled to not want to play with Sam, and Sam is entitled to feel hurt by Darren's decision not to play with him, but there are better ways to decline an invitation and express disappointment. The adult could teach them how to modulate their language to say what they each think and feel without hurting each other. For example, Darren could thank Sam for the invitation even in declining it, and offer the promise of another time to play ("No thank you Sam, let's play later"); Sam could show his disappointment that Darren doesn't want to play with him, but accept the hopeful gesture ("Okay I guess, come find me when you want to play.").

The same is true with siblings, with added layers of complexity because of their shared history. Bluma remembers the time she and Jessica were playing with their "doll house" -

a makeshift construction out of tissue boxes we carefully built atop a chair because we didn't actually own a Barbie house. Bluma was 8 and Jessica was 11. We'd just finished setting the scene to start playing with our dolls when the phone rang. It was one of Jessica's classmates inviting her to come over for a play date. Jessica jumped up and shot out of the room in her excitement to go to her friend's house, leaving Bluma alone with our toys, sad and upset. Losing a playmate is in itself a difficult thing for a child, but in the context of our relationship, for Bluma it felt even worse. By that point, our relationship was already marked by the cycle of violence, both physical and emotional, that we've described at length in this book. Watching Jessica abandon this brief moment of joy and peace in which we were about to have fun playing together felt all the more devastating for Bluma. It felt like another form of rejection from her older sister in the context of a relationship already defined by cycles of fighting and rejection.

Jessica did not do anything wrong by accepting her friend's invitation: it's good and healthy to bond with other children beyond your family circle. Kids love getting invited on playdates, and those kids left at home can feel bummed they don't have one to go to as well. However, what could have made this moment less painful for Bluma, and strengthened our friendship, would have been if someone had guided us through this transition. Jessica could have honestly and kindly told Bluma, "We'll play Barbies when I get back. Love you." That way, Bluma would feel hopeful and at ease. And Jessica could leave with a sense of relief that, upon her return, instead of a storm brewing, we would pick up where we left off.

Of course, we don't expect kids to conduct themselves like consular diplomats. And, this common exchange, inviting or declining play, continues to show up for our entire lives, as older children, teenagers and finally, as adults. Just substitute "play" for any other activity. It is vital to learn how to honor our thoughts and feelings while preserving the dignity of the relationship. Striking this balance is an ongoing endeavor as we continue to evolve throughout our lives. Our 8-year-old needs get replaced by more adult ones. As we learn to prioritize needs that fall under a variety of categories - "mine," "yours" and "ours" - we learn to occasionally delay our own sense of gratification to fulfill others' needs first. Usually, this works when you know or believe that at some point, after you've met someone's needs, yours will be met too. This is more difficult to do when you don't trust that your needs will be fulfilled.

Social psychologists say that the basis of successful relationships is reciprocity, or "tit-for-tat." Between siblings, couples and close friends, we learn to accept delayed gratification of our needs - a delayed "tit" for a "tat" - so long as at some point, we experience the exchange. No one likes to think we keep score in relationships…but we do…we ALL do. Imagine a new friendship. Raya comes over for coffee and sees you're out of your favorite kind. While at the store, Raya sees your brand, so she buys it for you. You're touched. As you get to know Raya, you realize she enjoys live music and in your IG feed you see a show coming to town that Raya might like, so you forward the link to her. These small acts are ways you're building your connection, which over time, creates trust. Without it, our

STEP 4 – LEARNING TO MOVE THROUGH CONFLICT

connection with other people wanes and eventually resentment builds, conflict follows, or the relationship ends.

However, a competing trend in our world today is to focus on the self (versus the relationship). Messages like 'speak your truth at all costs', 'focus on your own needs', and 'cut ties with people who don't add value to your life,' all encourage this philosophy. We promote these narratives as a **flex to feel aligned** with our tribe, hoping it will make us feel less alone. Yet, it's a contradiction in terms. We want to be the focus, yet without someone to see it, we lack validation. We can only venture as far as our culture considers acceptable, and that is an ever-moving target.

For example, the concept of being a "Karen" plowed through cultural norms, and by 2020, middle-aged, mainly white, women speaking their truth (usually complaining to management) became something to judge or cease. This gained traction because it showed a recognition of the imbalance between meeting my needs versus your needs. And now, when any woman has a complaint, she's considered a Karen (what about Kevins?). Our culture defines how to preserve our needs and others' needs with a certain expected etiquette.

As this relates to our sibling relationship; when you choose to address an issue with your sibling and "speak your truth" in a way that is not mindful of their feelings, you've Karen-ed the problem, which does not resolve anything. It actually creates more conflict. Not everyone can receive "your truth" openly, easily or authentically. And many of us aren't taught how to give others grace, or give the benefit of the doubt. We recommend you to reflect before you dive into conflict. How we share, when we share, and *if* we share are also factors we get to choose. It's important to learn how to share from a place of vulnerability, since that is where your **true** truth lies. It is also where your empowerment lives, and how others will feel safe to be open, authentic and vulnerable in turn. It is how real and long-term connection happens and growth flourishes. So, as you move through conflict with your sibling, consider when and how you'll share, and how to stay open to receive to ensure an optimal outcome, for me, you and us. The question is, how do I simultaneously meet my needs AND meet your needs too?

To start this evolution, ask yourself,

1. What is it about this moment that is important for me to understand, and what do I want to share with my sibling that will help us *both* feel seen and understood?

2. What are the values and needs I most want to cultivate in my sibling relationship now?

3. How can I communicate in a way that meets my needs, while also preserving and caring about my sibling's needs?

There's a difference between word-vomiting everything that's on your mind, as opposed to taking a beat to think of how best to express what you need. This is a shift, from impulsively reacting, to consciously communicating. It's like giving the Karens of the world a hug, while also supporting the management's circumstances. It broadens what we imagine is possible - that we can both be valued, both be appreciated, and both get our needs acknowledged.

Using the Prime Directive helped us develop the ability to hold the other's perspectives with as much care and compassion as our own. The Prime Directive is like the parts of a watch, and Memory Sharing is the mechanism that makes it run. A watch without a power source is just an accessory. Memory sharing gave us that mechanism to bring to life a healthy way of having a new relationship together. We learned that having a different perspective doesn't cancel out the other - two feelings can be true at the same time. We practiced this over and over and over, until it spilled into the rest of the way we communicate together. And we watched this enrich our communication in other relationships too. So, although some might have called us Karens, back in the day (maybe not so far back), we are now evolved enough to see value in Karens and their counterparts.

Perspective Taking is integrating the Prime Directive and Memory Sharing to strengthen your ability to hold space for other perspectives, while also honoring your own.

There have been times when we are stuck or blocked because, let's face it, we've had a lot longer to be who we *were* than who we have become. So, we had to figure out ways to address these temporary moments and find a path through. We use the Prime Directive to stay curious and open. Recently, after a particularly frustrating conflict, we realized that we couldn't move through it easily, so we put it to the side. We stayed in contact, talked about other things (Shoot the Shit), but gave the feelings time to settle.

In the past, after an intense conflict, we would never have respected each other's boundaries. We would have forced a process we weren't ready for, and it would have erupted between us and disrupted our entire family system. It might have been months or years before we would have ever spoken, and even then, we would have still been looking to be right. Now, although there was an awareness that something needed to be processed, we stayed whole, connected and committed until we were both ready to figure it out. We are driven by the commitment that our relationship is *fundamental and non-disposable*. We've learned to trust that taking space *isn't an abandonment*; it is in fact sometimes necessary for us to gain clarity.

This chapter is about how to navigate these temporary standstills in new ways, so your relationship reaches a mutual understanding together, and continues to evolve, grow and flourish. **Growth flows from connection, and through conflict**.

Here's a real-world example with 2 adult siblings:

Alicia and Sasha were planning a trip together. Alicia needed Sasha to let her know by Friday, which days Sasha could travel so that Alicia could request time off from work. Friday came without Sasha sharing dates, so Alicia called Sasha Friday morning and left a voicemail, following up with a text message, asking Sasha for an answer by the end of the day. Sasha called her back on Monday. Alicia lays into Sasha, "You never pick up the phone when I call; you're so selfish and don't give a shit about me!" Sasha responds, "I never answer my phone? Well, you're a baby and call too often and can't sort things out without other people's help." Alicia hangs up, their trip is canceled. They don't talk for weeks, with the tension hanging onto their insides, distracting them from being present in their lives. The negativity hangover spews into their other relationships.

We can all relate to this.
Jessica and Bluma fell into this communication pattern quite often. Once starting this journey together, we changed our pattern by slowwwwwing the process down. Tension is uncomfortable, so we tried to avoid it, yet staying in it a little longer stretches you to realize that you can handle more than you thought, and grow your pattern into something evolved and elevated, together. We started acknowledging what was happening RIGHT NOW (and not lumping all the past feelings into one moment). We stayed present to share the feelings and needs we're having by using phrases such as: "This is making me uncomfortable" "I'm being triggered;" or requesting, "Can you say that differently?" And, we spoke these with a consciousness to our tone, our words and our intensity to remain kind, gentle, and open.

Alicia Reframe

Sasha says: "Alicia, I want to stay open to hear you, so would you say that differently please, because it makes me withdraw from you when you accuse me that way, and it's triggering for *me*." Alicia tries again, "Fine. I'm bummed you didn't get back to me on Friday when I called because I needed to sort out my vacation days from work, and it ended up creating difficulties for *me*." Starting this way, Alicia gets her feelings heard and understood by Sasha. And, by sharing her frustrations about something concrete, as opposed to first focusing on her sister's character, Alicia addresses the specific issue that is interfering now and, together, they can find a solution to avoid repeating this unhelpful pattern.

> *In trying to protect ourselves individually, Jessica and Bluma realized that avoiding being wrong only escalates conflict. The Prime Directive (Chapter 6) moved us through an impasse like this; specifically, "Be curious, Be compassionate, Seek understanding" to identify the breakdown in our communication. This opened an awareness of one of our default patterns and shifted our energy together, toward forgiveness, repair and connection. The Memory Sharing process bolstered trust in valuing each perspective to find our own authentic voices, and have compassion for our part in each other's pain within this moment.*

Sasha Reframe

Sasha says, "That *is* annoying. I'm sorry. I was in meetings all day and really didn't have time to talk. And then I forgot to follow up…and that made you feel ignored and not prioritized. For me, I get overwhelmed by the pressure to respond right away to your calls and messages, and so I also kinda avoid it. Let's figure out a new way we can communicate together so you get what you need, and I do too." This pivots the pattern between them so they can work out a system where Alicia can communicate when something is a more urgent matter (and needs to be addressed soon), versus something trivial that can be minimally acknowledged (where a 👍 will suffice). Then, Alicia feels valued and prioritized. And for Sasha, she now has clarity about what is urgent for Alicia and what can be tabled during her work day, leaving Sasha to feel less pressured to respond to every message. Sasha now feels valued and prioritized as well.

Feeling like you fundamentally respect your sibling is an elixir to pains - past, present and future. However, feeling like you fundamentally disrespect your sibling, or feeling morally superior or even disgusted by them, is a paradigm that undermines the positive rapport you share. For us, the superiority-inferiority cha-cha had long been our dance. It is hard to feel vulnerable, open and safe when you feel judged, inadequate and repulsive. We had felt this way toward each other for so long, it was hard to imagine feeling any other way. Right from the beginning, we intuitively knew we needed to build a culture of appreciation into our adult sibling relationship. We saw that sharing gratitude was a remedy to our negative patterns. We chose to have an attitude of gratitude as the flavor of our culture as sisters. It's what we mean when we say we give each other "grace." We give each other the benefit of the doubt, we appreciate our sibling's struggle, and we are grateful we are in a place within our relationship where we can help, support and show up for each other. Shifting from the superiority-inferiority cha-cha to the gratitude-appreciation waltz slowed our conflicts down and made them easier to dissolve.

Another family relic for us, "cut-n-run", was an attempt to remove vagus triggers (sweaty palms, narrow vision, body tension). It shut down the process and disengaged us from each other, leaving us alone with the conflict. Most conversations would end with one of us hanging up or walking off. It reinforced the feeling that we couldn't handle each other - it was too much, and it was going to combust. We hadn't ever learned how to emotionally regulate and bring our hearts and minds back to baseline. *So, we taught ourselves how.* We incorporated ways to physiologically self soothe and calm our nervous systems down: breathing, grounding, changing your state (Chapter 6)...all so we were able to stay present and address the conflict together.

We've spoken about breathing and grounding in, but changing your state is a bold way to dramatically shift your mind & body energy. Often when we are stuck in a conflict and can't find the words, we will say "get up!" and we rock out to "The Greatest Showman" or "Celebration", pushing a dance party into the tension of the moment. We wiggle & jiggle, we boogie and groove, we pound our chests and bellow out mantras of strength and fortitude and self-love. It's the fast-track to getting us to a baseline that allows for constructive and creative speaking, listening and processing - keeping us grounded, centered and focused on the new groove we're grinding through and over old pathways. Another useful example is that one of us will say, "Can I give you a hug," or one of us will hug the other one, to change our state and shift us back into a loving connection.

So, how can you move through conflict with grace? Our biggest advice is to stay curious. If your sibling says something that's upsetting to you, get curious and understand why. Ask them a question. Reflect inwardly. Slow down the process. *There's no finish line*: you don't have to race through the healing process. Every conflict takes you further down the road of reconciliation. Staying curious will allow your brain to kick into creative problem-solving mode, instead of hunkering down into fight, flight or freeze mode. In the previous chapter, we outlined our Memory Sharing choreography, in which you each share your recollections or certain memories, acknowledge how you each made the other feel, and forgive each other for the parts you played in each other's pain. It can take as long as you need. *Trust that you will both find your pace* – even if it means taking breaks to give your heart, mind and soul a chance to soothe, reset and re-engage.

Keep consciously breathing! Take breaks! Communicate with your sibling! Remember that you're making huge strides every time you realize you're heading towards conflict. Surrender to the conflict, engage with one another with the tools you have learned. You may not always be able to avoid feeling some tension, but noticing it happening is already a huge step forward. It means you're on your way toward healthier and more constructive ways to move through conflict. Keep going. You are creating alignment in living a more fulfilling life. You're doing great.

CHAPTER 10

Step 5 - Cultural Fusion

Before we jump into the next step of the healing process, we want you to give yourself a huge pat on the back for coming this far - for giving yourself and your sibling a chance to accomplish something extraordinary. This takes commitment, and we're so proud of you for doing it. So seriously, get yourself a celebratory treat. Do a victory dance. You deserve it.

At this point in the process, you will have spent time identifying your archetypes, sharing your past pain points and discussing your roles in them, and improving your conflict dialogue. You'll have taken responsibility and forgiven each other. You'll be moving away from feeling like you should always have the moral high ground in an argument or need to air all of your thoughts and feelings, no matter how they impact your sibling. You'll be focusing on authenticity instead of accuracy. The Prime Directive will have become your sacred scripture: you will be committed to being a witness, and being remorseful, forgiving, curious, compassionate and understanding.

You'll have been breathing through the hard parts, and celebrating the progress you make each time you two meet. Because you are progressing - even on the days you feel emotionally raw or frustrated. You're doing it.

We suggest you spend about four weeks really concentrating on Steps 1-4, though of course, if it feels right, we encourage you to extend this phase of the process for as long as you need. This is your journey.

Once you feel like you and your sibling have hit a stride - that you've mastered the Memory Sharing choreography and refined your conflict dialogue skills - it will then be time to move on to the next phase. And that's Step 5: cultural fusion.

As we've mentioned before, it's vitally important you keep the first part of the work - Steps 1-4 - *between you and your sibling at first*. You're building a new house together, and for the duration of the time you're laying out the new structure, the house will be fragile. You'll only want the builders on site, and that's you and your sibling. Inviting a bunch of other people in while the walls and beams aren't properly holding up each floor could be dangerous for everyone involved. You need to keep other people out until it's sturdy.

Once you've completed it, though, you'll want your loved ones to see it. You'll have spent all this time, energy and effort, and poured all this love into making something you're proud of. You'll want to invite the rest of your family in.

That's what cultural fusion is about. In this chapter, we'll discuss how, once you and your sibling have made significant progress in repairing your relationship—or are well on your way—you can begin to share that work with other family members. Your adult sibling relationship is renewed. Bringing your other family members into the fold not only shows them the fruits of your labor, but also fosters a way forward to integrate your new sibling relationship into your broader family structure.

Once again, we want to stress the importance of waiting for the right time to do this. You should not rush it. Sharing your work with the rest of your family - your parents and other siblings - in the early days of your work adds stress at a time when you and your sibling are still building trust and understanding between the two of you. Your parents and other siblings might doubt your ability to repair your relationship, like ours did. If all they've ever known and seen of the two of you is strife, they'll have a fixed image in their minds of who you are together. They'll think of each of you as your archetype. As we explained in Chapter 7, the archetype your family assigns you is an incredibly powerful force. It shapes how your parents and other siblings engage with and respond to you. And it trains *you* to behave in a way that matches their expectations. In the early days of the healing process, while you're still identifying and understanding your archetypes and working on extracting the essence that is 'you,' and releasing the aspects that aren't, you absolutely want to avoid putting yourselves in situations where you are both being pinned to those roles. It would be too easy to fall back into them. You don't want your parents' and other siblings' preconceptions of either of you to undo all the hard work you're doing. And, they wouldn't even know that what they were doing was hurting your progress.

Earlier, we compared the healing process to a house under construction. Here's another way of illustrating it. When you start healing your relationship, those early days are like planting a new seed. Your previous relationship as siblings is part of an age-old family tree whose roots run deep into the ground and branches extend high into the sky. It's home to generations and generations of family members whose fantastic jumble of genes and experiences - including the transgenerational histories and legacy burdens we discussed in Chapter 3 - flow straight into you and your sibling. To start anew, you have to plant a new tree. In the early days, while this new tree is a mere seedling in the ground, you have to watch over it carefully. You have to make sure it's getting enough water and sunlight to grow, but not too much - you don't want to drown it. It's delicate and fragile. It's getting stronger by the day, but it's still tender - and much more so than the full-fledged tree that is the rest of your family. Their tree is strong and fixed and has weathered many storms. It could easily smother your small seedling at this point. You have to wait until your seed has grown roots and can stand on its own before you share it with your family.

We knew this instinctively when we embarked on this journey, so we agreed to wait to tell the rest of our family about our work. We said we would consult each other before delivering any news. But then something unexpected happened.

A few weeks into our process, our mom and sister visited Bluma in Israel. It was a lovely but difficult reunion: our mom fell ill and had to go to the hospital. It was frightening and emotions ran high. When our mom was released, the three of them - Bluma, our mom and younger sister Sara - met in a café. While they sipped coffee and picked at sandwiches, Bluma suddenly felt like not telling them about our work - this transformative experience that was now so central to her life - was a betrayal of the love and trust they bore each other. Our mom had just been through a life-threatening situation, so big changes were on their minds. How could she not tell them about her own transformation? Bluma's loyalties were divided. On the one hand, she wanted to honor her agreement with Jessica and protect the seedling of our new, burgeoning sibling relationship. On the other hand, she needed to open up to our mom, a pillar in her life, or risk feeling dishonest and alienated from her. So Bluma made the call. She took a deep breath and told our mom and sister Sara she had an announcement to make. And she told them we were working on healing our relationship. Fresh out of the hospital, our mom's face was already a little paler than her usual rosy countenance, and now the color she did have seemed to completely drain. "Well, good luck with that," she answered.

This is clearly a negative reaction. Our mom didn't mean any harm, of course; she was responding to shocking news that didn't track with her lived experience. All she'd ever seen and known of her two oldest daughters was conflict and strife. Bluma telling our mom that we were fixing our relationship and actively aiming to become close was like announcing she was moving to Mars. So yeah, good luck with that.

It's hard for families to accept that one member - never mind two - has changed. Families are like a fragile ecosystem in which everyone has a particular function. If anyone decides to start behaving differently, it forces everyone to shift gears and adapt or react to that change. Imagine a family like a group of people all holding a heavy table above their heads. The table's weight is evenly distributed among all the lifters, and as long as everyone stays where they are and doesn't move, the table stays balanced. But if one person decides they want to step away from the table, or switch sides, suddenly everyone is forced to adjust to keep the table aloft. Each individual might have to find a new place or carry a bit more weight. It can be tense and a bit uncomfortable, but it's the only way to find equilibrium.

You see this in families in which one member needs to make a drastic change. For example, say Mia, after years of struggling with her drinking, is diagnosed with alcohol addiction and decides to attend meetings and stay away from wine and liquor at family events. This can be a tough shift for the rest of the family. First off, Mia might seem very different to them. Until it became a full-out problem, they loved Mia's fun energy at gatherings; she was the life of the party, the one who always enlivened a Sunday night dinner and kept otherwise dull board games fun. Now, sober Mia is much more subdued and introspective, and part of the family misses her liveliness. And then there's the fact that Mia has asked them to be careful about leaving alcohol around the house, and be sensitive about drinking in front of her. The family might be supportive of Mia's decision to quit and attend AA, but they might be more resistant about changing their own habits. They're not problem drinkers, they might think to themselves, so why should they have to change? We'll delve more into family ecosystems in Chapter 11.

When Bluma told our mom and sister Sara that we were changing our relationship, along with their disbelief, they probably experienced a certain sense of unease and fear regarding how this would change the rest of the family dynamic. All they'd ever known was that Bluma was part of their nucleus, and Jessica was not. Would trips like this, with just the three of them, still be possible in this theoretical future world in which Bluma and Jessica were also close? As we explained in Chapter 4, the familiar feels safe, even if it isn't right. Jessica as the Black Sheep was what felt familiar and normal in our family. Bluma announcing that we were upending the status quo in our family pattern meant we were all embarking into the unknown - not just us, but them too.

When you're in the early days of healing your adult sibling relationship, this kind of external negative feedback can be seriously destabilizing. If you, like Bluma, value your other family members' opinions, it can be extremely difficult not to let it affect you. Thankfully, because of her training as a psychologist, Bluma was able to see and understand our mom's reaction ("Good luck with that.") as a normal and fear-based response, and reply, simply, "I understand your concern, thank you." Our mom's reaction did not impact Bluma's resolve to keep working with Jessica. But it easily could have. And while this was not Bluma's intention, by telling our mom, she was perpetuating a toxic family pattern: she and our mom were in cahoots while Jessica was left out.

Bluma knew she had to tell Jessica. The next time we met on Zoom, Bluma explained what had happened. It was tough for Jessica to take this information in. She felt raw and anxious and upset. Bluma telling our mom about us was a betrayal of our trust. At the same time, Jessica was not surprised. She knew that Bluma's connection with our mom and sister was stronger than our connection at that point and that, inevitably, Bluma would feel pulled in their direction. For the first time since she could remember, Jessica felt open to hearing Bluma's take, even as it hurt her. Bluma explained that she had indeed been torn between honoring two relationships at the same time, two relationships which, historically, had been at odds. And just as it was hard for Jessica to hear this, Bluma admitted that it was hard for her to say this out loud. Just as Jessica was resisting an old pattern - reacting angrily after feeling shut out by our family - Bluma was also doing her best not to repeat another pattern - withholding information from Jessica in order to spare her feelings and avoid a conflict. It was an incredibly difficult moment for us both that could have splintered us and undone all of our progress. We both felt this strong pull to act as we always had: to go into defense mode and stonewall each other, to "cut and run." We didn't this time. We talked it out. Acknowledging what was happening, what was being triggered from our past, and what it felt like now, gave us the opportunity to not succumb to those pulls, and to build something new.

Ultimately, Bluma telling our mom about our process in the early days did not derail our progress. You might also be thinking that, since you are close with your mom or dad, or another sibling, you would like to loop them in too. And maybe it would be fine. But we strongly recommend you hold off. As you can see in our example, bringing other family members in early on inevitably creates some tension, either between you and those other family members, or between you and your sibling. From the bottom of our hearts, we urge you to be patient.

Once the timing is right, gently introduce your family of origin - the family you were born into, that strong and fixed family tree - to your new family - the one you're building with your adult sibling now. Take it as slow as you need. You don't have to arrange a big family meeting or intervention of any kind. You could start by having a coffee with a parent and letting them know, then later telling your other siblings over the phone. Nothing needs to feel intimidating or dramatic. You make your announcement in whichever way makes sense to you. If your family sounds shocked or confused, don't be offended by their surprise; just let the news sink in. Hold onto your confidence about your mission and success. Accept that it may take the rest of your family, who have not witnessed your progress, some time to accept and understand that you and your sibling have healed, and so the relationship has changed. And give them grace while they adapt to that change, and perhaps change themselves.

What we want to achieve with Step 5 is cultural fusion - not combustion. We want the whole family to benefit from your growth as siblings. And the best way we believe you can achieve this is leading by example.

As we've explained, the longstanding dynamic in our family was for Bluma, our mom and our other siblings to be in cahoots while Jessica was left on the outside. When our mother married our step-father Joe, our family pattern at the time was what it had always been, and Joe experienced our mom's relationship with Jessica in its toxic pattern. When he learned we had begun to heal our relationship, he had strong reservations about the impact it could have on our mother. Bluma sent a letter to him to set the expectation for our intentions:

Dearest Stepfather~

A very engaging intro, I know, but I want to frame it that way, just this once.

I have already said to you before that you are a gift to me, my siblings and all our children. You have given us, albeit late in the game, a 'restorative emotional experience' - loving fatherly attention and devotion we have all hungered for. You are blessed with your own loving, adoring children, and grandchildren - yet, you made room in your heart to include us too, and you do it all so gracefully! You share your love with a full heart, always caring about our troubles, always jumping in our joy! It is truly God's Gift!

It is expected that, as my mother's soulmate, guardian angel, and best friend, you would have <u>warranted</u> concerns of how engaging in Peace Talks with Jessica and me could impact my mother's joy and well-being.

We were also concerned!! So from the start, we created one overarching, cultural expectation - the Prime Directive:

"Be a witness. Be Forgiving. Be Remorseful. Be curious. Be understanding."

We are like archeologists, combing through each relic, dusting off debris, cataloging its meaning and relevance...and then, carefully integrating it within our relationship.

We have found that this releases the tension, and replaces it with compassion. Honest to goodness!

It is emotional, but not unhealthy. We are not blaming, disparaging or criticizing. We are seeking closeness, understanding and harmony...and we do this by exploring **together***, using our Prime Directive as our compass.*

Michelle will be supported, encouraged and cared for throughout this journey, by us, and of course, always, by you, Thank God! I hope this helps put your heart and mind at ease.

With love,

Bluma

Although significant change came quickly, our mother and Joe would often wonder on phone calls how our newfound friendship was holding up, their skepticism lingering as a quiet relic of the past. For years, our relationship as healed siblings existed mostly in conversations and small moments, unseen by the larger family. Our family, after all, was scattered across the globe, making full family gatherings a rare occasion. But eventually, the time came when we would all be together again.

Before that first family gathering, we made a conscious effort to support each other, agreeing on ways to reinforce our bond. As familiar dynamics began to emerge, Bluma ensured—through both words and actions—that Jessica was not left on the outside. If she noticed Jessica looking frustrated, she would take her hand or squeeze her shoulder in a simple but powerful show of solidarity. These subtle yet deliberate gestures signaled our transformation, and in time, our family of origin took notice. Slowly, our mother, step-father, other siblings, and even our cousins, began to shift their own behavior, reflecting the beautiful change they saw between us.

As Jessica and Bluma began seeking endorsements for our book, our stepfather Joe eagerly volunteered to write an endorsement:

> *I have known Bluma & Jessica for the past 12 years. Until 5 years ago, their relationship was what I would describe as toxic. I never thought anything would change that. But 5 years ago they committed to the methods they developed in their book and miraculously they are now friends. They are now committed to spreading their methodology to other siblings who want to change as well. Impressive.*
> Joseph Mezistrano, M.D.

In some cases, certain family members might not embrace the change - and that's OK too. People who don't seem inclined to see you or your sibling in a new light may have their own reasons for not doing so. It may be a boundary they're setting. We encourage you to return to the Prime Directive and respect their decision with compassion and curiosity.

Cultural fusion is about healthy acceptance. You get to choose to respond differently to your parents when they behave the same way they always have with you. We modeled a different way to be for our whole family. Today, they see the strength we have created. They accept it and see the benefits of what we've done. Conscious or unconscious attempts to split us don't work.

CHAPTER 11

Step 6 - Managing Your Evolution (Wash, Rinse, Repeat)

Here we are. You've made it to Step 6 of the process. You've come a long way since you first opened this book. You may have started out thinking that fixing your sibling relationship would be hard. Maybe you wondered if it would even be possible. By now, we hope you've realized how easy it can be. **Like flipping a switch.**

Recently, a friend of Jessica's asked her to blow up a mattress. Jessica has worked as the CEO of her own company; she knows how to get business done. But for some reason, at that moment, being responsible for that task felt overwhelming. She didn't know how the mattress was meant to be blown up; she hadn't seen it or read the instructions. She would have rather passed. But she took a breath and walked down into the basement, where the mattress was folded up on the floor. And that's when she saw that it inflated automatically. All she had to do was switch on a button.

Just like Jessica feeling nervous about blowing up the mattress before she saw it, deciding to heal your adult sibling relationship may feel daunting before you actually start the process. The fear and anticipation of trying something new is almost always more daunting than the thing itself. Just like any new project or activity - learning to ride a bike or picking up a new instrument - the most challenging part is deciding to do it. It's choosing to open your mind, invest the time, and face the unknown.

We have all had the experience of clinging to what's familiar even if it's unhealthy; we discussed this at length in Chapter 4. So congratulations for facing the uncertainty! We're so proud of you for looking it square in the face, and grabbing hold of your sibling's hand to venture into it. By taking this leap, you've started walking down a new path paved with love, compassion, understanding and joy.

We were shocked by how quick and simple it was to reframe our sibling dynamic. What started out looking like a mountain we had to conquer proved to be just a switch we had to flip.

This is just the beginning of the road. We're so excited for you to carry all the knowledge and practices you've learned in "I'm Right You're Stupid" into your everyday life. That's what this chapter is all about. It's not an ending. This chapter is really a beginning. A new beginning for you and your sibling; a new road the two of you can travel together, side by side, hand in hand.

In the previous chapter, Step 5 of the process, we discussed how to introduce your family of origin into your process and model for them your changed dynamic. In this chapter, we're going to talk about how to extend that process beyond your family circle and into your broader community - your friendships, your relationships with colleagues or classmates, your romantic relationships, and other acquaintances and strangers.

Right now, it's time to let go of the coping mechanisms and maladaptive strategies that no longer serve you. Today, embrace the new space, energy and love you have within you to engage more curiously and compassionately with the world around you. It's about embracing beauty and abundance. So let's get going!

At this stage, it is safe to say you grasp this all too well: your sibling relationship impacts every other relationship in your life. The fear and mistrust we experienced as sisters permeated our other relationships - the significant ones, but also the ones on the periphery of our lives, including the strangers and acquaintances we ran into on the street or in the grocery store. Before we did this work, we struggled to emotionally regulate - to self soothe - and creatively approach conflict, because those tense situations sent us straight back to the emotional and mental spaces we inhabited during our childhood. They were dead ringers for all the chaos and confusion we experienced growing up: the fighting and bullying we inflicted on each other, compounded by our parents' inability to constructively intervene and mitigate our arguments. It was a never-ending cycle of blow ups with no repairs. We never knew when the next explosion was coming, so we were always on the lookout. This state of hypervigilance followed us everywhere. We couldn't switch it off the second we walked out our front door, so it followed us to school, to the mall, to the gym and wherever else we went, as kids and then as adults. It made us *expect* conflict from others, and react disproportionately to small triggers. We didn't know that our outgrown reactions were not based in reality, but in our memories of the past. We were chained to them.

By working together, we tore through those chains. By diving back into our past and Memory Sharing, we got to see how little Bluma and little Jessica were set up to see each other as competitors instead of allies from forces beyond our control, including transgenerational history and the roles we were assigned. We began to understand that when we approached each other with curiosity and compassion, we could pierce through the anger that had punctuated so much of our history and see it for what it was: a plea for love and acceptance.

Processing our past trauma together liberated us from the hold it had over us. Before we did this work, our reactions to each other - and to the people around us - often felt out of our control. It felt like our interactions with others triggered an ancient mechanism that set off a whole range of physical and emotional responses, often leaving us flustered and bewildered. That's not the case anymore. We have a presence of mind now. We're no longer reactive; now we're responsive. Reacting is knee-jerk. Responding is thoughtful and measured. Now, when we disagree with each other, or with others, we work to understand where the other is coming from - what their perspective is - in a collaborative way. And that's the game changer. The goal is not to never fight, because conflict happens. The goal is to approach conflict with curiosity and compassion.

And that's how we've rebranded, both as individuals and as sisters.

Of course, personal growth is an ongoing evolution. It's about changing your mindset, and then carrying your newfound wisdom forward with you.

Breaking the bonds of your unhealthy sibling relationship is like creating a new ecosystem. In biology, an ecosystem is a group of living things that interact with each other and rely on each other for survival. For example, in a pond, fish, frogs, plants, and insects interact in the water and on the banks of the pond, relying on each other for food and shelter. Families have their own ecosystems. Remember our table analogy from the previous chapter? The family ecosystem has every member carrying a heavy table over their heads. The table stays up as long as everyone stays where they are. There's balance. There's structure. But that doesn't mean everyone is happy or comfortable. Maybe one person is straining under the weight while two other people barely feel it. The person who's struggling may want to move or readjust, but no one else wants them to, since that would throw the existing balance off. The system is not perfect, but as long as the table remains aloft, it seems to be working.

Now imagine the dissatisfied family member does break away. If they do that, if they let go of the table and step away from the rest of the family, the whole system collapses. The table may fall to the ground. The family has to figure something new out to get the table back in the air. They need to decide on a new weight distribution arrangement among the remaining family members, or agree to an adjustment so the dissatisfied member will come back. This is often an uncomfortable moment, and one that is full of possibility. This is called "the window of vitality." It's an incredible phenomenon in which, out of the chaos of the old system's destruction, a new system can emerge. The window of vitality is a moment of amazing potential and creativity when something totally new can come to life. However, if a new system doesn't take hold, the old system is likely to be restored. We cannot *thrive* under chaos. We need systems.

When you and your sibling dismantle your previous relationship, you step into the window of vitality. That's what this whole process - Growing Up Your Sibling Relationship - is helping you through. You're creating a new system under which to live and grow. Your new sibling culture is your new ecosystem. And it's a way of being that extends far beyond your sibling relationship. It shapes how you operate in the world in all of your other relationships. Since this is a new system, it's a work in progress, and you might still feel the pull of the old system. That's why it's important to be mindful of the new system. You have to honor it, and you may need to tweak it when necessary, as your circumstances change. It's fluid. To live by this new guiding principle, you have to wash, rinse, repeat.

The good news is that, just like switching on the automatic button of Jessica's mattress, it's easy! It's a choice you make and a guide by which to live your life. Keeping the process alive fills you with a sense of balance. That's what it's done for us.

So without further ado, we want to share a few tips on how to manage your evolution as adult siblings with a newfound perspective on your past and newly healed relationship.

An essential part of managing your evolution is returning to the Memory Sharing process to work through conflict. We designed Memory Sharing as an integral step for adult sibling healing. However, we quickly realized how well it applies to other conflictual moments, between you and your sibling, after you've healed your relationship, and also with other people. It works as a brilliant model for how to deal with conflict generally. You don't have to go through the whole choreography we outlined in Chapter 8, and you don't have to delve into your deepest childhood memories with total strangers. What you can do is share your version of events and acknowledge your role in someone else's experience. At heart, Memory Sharing is about processing experiences, and that's how two people with different perspectives are understood. You work on being curious and compassionate to understand the divergence between your two views; this is about sharing perspectives, not convincing, not being accurate, not being right (or stupid). It's about finding ways for you to preserve and restore your connection. Keeping this process alive, when you experience conflict within your sibling relationship, and outside of it, will help you stay on a path of growth.

Another important part of managing your evolution is learning to decide when you should approach conflict - with compassion and curiosity, of course - and when you should just let it go. Memory Sharing is your guide to working through conflict in a healthy and constructive fashion, but you don't always need to go there. Sometimes, when you feel a rush of frustration or sadness, the best option is to allow that wave of emotion to wash over you and retreat like a sea at low tide. As we explained in Chapter 4, you can't stop yourself from getting triggered. If you grew up with sibling conflict (which, if you have a sibling, you have), you are going to get triggered by other people when you find yourself in conflictive situations that are rooted in your unresolved sibling history. You will feel that unconscious command to fight, flight or freeze. That's beyond your control. But what is very much within your control is how you choose to respond to those triggers. You learned to control your reactions in Chapters 5 and 9, in which we provided tips and strategies to emotionally regulate and refine your conflict dialogue skills. You can ground yourself; you can take a few deep breaths; you can take a break and return to the conflict later when you feel more calm. You can train yourself to notice the early signs of stress your body emits when your mind feels overwhelmed, and you can soothe your body.

Choosing to consciously turn away from conflict isn't running away from it. When you feel yourself grow tense, a part of you is - or various parts of you are - trying to get certain needs met, like finding safety or avoiding pain. Some of these parts may be much younger versions of yourself that feel like they weren't properly seen and heard when you were involved in arguments, and want to be acknowledged and understood now. This is what we discussed in Chapter 8 when we talked about the different parts of you that have to be integrated in order to make you feel whole. When unresolved pain gets triggered, a protective mechanism kicks into gear and tries to repress the memories of that pain so that they're not on the forefront of your mind. This mechanism is trying to be helpful - it just wants you to move forward and get on with your life without looking back. The problem is that you can't make those memories disappear. By pushing them down in your psyche, you're actually making them fight harder to be heard. They'll keep bubbling up to the surface of your consciousness, intruding on your everyday life in difficult and complicated ways, until they're integrated into your sense of self. Accepting those parts - hearing them out - is the only way to truly be whole.

After processing your past sibling pain, those parts will likely have grown quieter. They did for us. They stopped disturbing us because they realized we were finally listening to them. But those parts don't disappear. They can't - they're part of you! They're a part of you which you should cherish and love because they've made you who you are today. However, those parts of you don't have to drive your actions today, because you are driving now and they are your passengers.

So when you feel yourself grow frustrated, stop and take stock of what your mind and body are asking of you. What do they want? Acknowledge the needs that are coming up and try to understand where they're coming from. Are some of them from a place, deep down, that used to feel scared, angry or neglected because you didn't feel accepted or protected as a child? Realize that you no longer inhabit the same situation, and gently comfort that part of you by taking a few deep breaths, or grounding yourself, or whatever you need to do to self soothe, and in so doing reminding this part of you that it's OK. You're

OK. You're not a child anymore, it's not happening to you now, and you're an adult who's got this!

So listen to yourself. That voice, the part of you that needed to be heard before you embarked on your adult sibling healing, is still present, but it no longer needs to be the loudest voice within you. As you get better at listening and paying attention to the parts of you that were exiled with unmet needs, they will begin to feel seen and heard and trust that you will keep listening and remain engaged and integrated. The purpose of that loud voice was to protect you, and you have to love that voice and thank it for being so dedicated to protecting you. Now that that voice knows you're aware of it - that you're accountable - it can release its burden.

Think of it this way. You don't fit in the same pair of shoes you wore when you were 8 years old. You don't wear the same clothes you did when you were 10. You outgrew those things. You have also outgrown coping styles and defense mechanisms you created when you were young. Acknowledge and appreciate that part of yourself, and then relieve it of its duty. Allow it to finally rest.

Something remarkable will happen then. One day, probably when you least suspect it, you'll notice something different about you. This revelation will not be loud. You won't hear any trumpets or fanfare, there won't be any thunder or lightning. But like a flower slowly blooming and stretching toward the sun, you'll notice a certain quiet. A sense of peace. A vastness.

For so long, you were unaware you were carrying around a heavy backpack on your shoulders filled with unprocessed trauma and obstructive coping mechanisms to get you through the day. Now the weight's been lifted. The mental space it took up is free. There's so much more room for other thoughts, feelings and possibilities.

Picture it this way. Before you did this work, you were like a fish in an aquarium, constantly having to navigate through or around a trove of plants, decorations, castles and algae. All of this took up so much space, you had no choice but to think about it and deal with it. It was your world. Processing your past trauma and healing your sibling relationship got rid of all those plants and contraptions. Now you can swim freely. You can think. You can be yourself.

Adult sibling healing allows you to become the true you. Your past no longer controls you. You get to decide how you relate to the world around you.

That's another key to managing your evolution. It's listening to yourself, the true and unobstructed you, and deciding how exactly you want to engage with the people around you; how interdependent you want to be. Life is all about interdependence. It's about finding the right balance between being happy and solid on our own - being independent - and knowing when to lean on other people when you need to - being dependent. Because being fully independent or fully dependent are both untenable choices that lack balance. If you're fully independent, you turn away from the world and don't have to worry about being vulnerable with other people, which is messy and scary, but you are completely alone, which is anathema to the human experience. If you're fully dependent, you don't have to worry about making any tough decisions, since they're being made for you, but you miss out on being a sovereign, autonomous human being, which is also wildly important to a healthy sense of self. We all need a bit of both.

What we all need is to learn the art of interdependence. We each get to decide how vulnerable and open to others we are willing to be while still holding onto ourselves. That delicate space is where growth and empowerment takes place.

We've talked about continuums in this book: the sibling continuum in Chapter 2 and the parental continuum in Chapter 3. The balance between dependence and independence is the third continuum we call the Holon Continuum. This one is all about your ecosystem, or your community. Remember our discussion of ecosystems earlier in this chapter? How they need to have an established structure and system in order to work? In biology, this relationship is called a holarchy, based on the word Holon, derived from the Greek word ὄλον (pronounced óyon) for "part-whole" and the Hebrew word חולן (pronounced holon) for "a grain of sand." A holarchy is about how parts need independence but cannot exist without the organization they are operating within. And a grain of sand is the perfect illustration of interdependence. A single particle of sand, on its own, can seem insignificant. It's minuscule. However, if it gets in your eye, you damn well feel it. It's sneakily powerful. And as part of a beach or a dune in the Sahara, it's obviously exceptional and immense. It can rise up in a cloud as part of a sandstorm. Sand, or *holon*, is special because of its dependence and independence. Because it is singular and also plural. Just like you.

We'd like you to take a look at the Holon Continuum (page 194) below and think about where you fall on it from day to day. How dominant is your self-system, or your sense of independence? How dominant is your social system, or your sense of dependence on others? How well do you find a balance between each one, and experience interdependence? How present are feelings or experiences of cooperation and support? Competition and sabotage? In Chapter 2 and 3 we shared with you ways to think about using the continuums. Remember that once you expand your perspective, and view of yourself and your world, you expand the space you have for the layers, the degrees, and the multiplicity of who you really were, who you actually are now and who you will become. This is what the continuum offers. A dilated view of your reality.

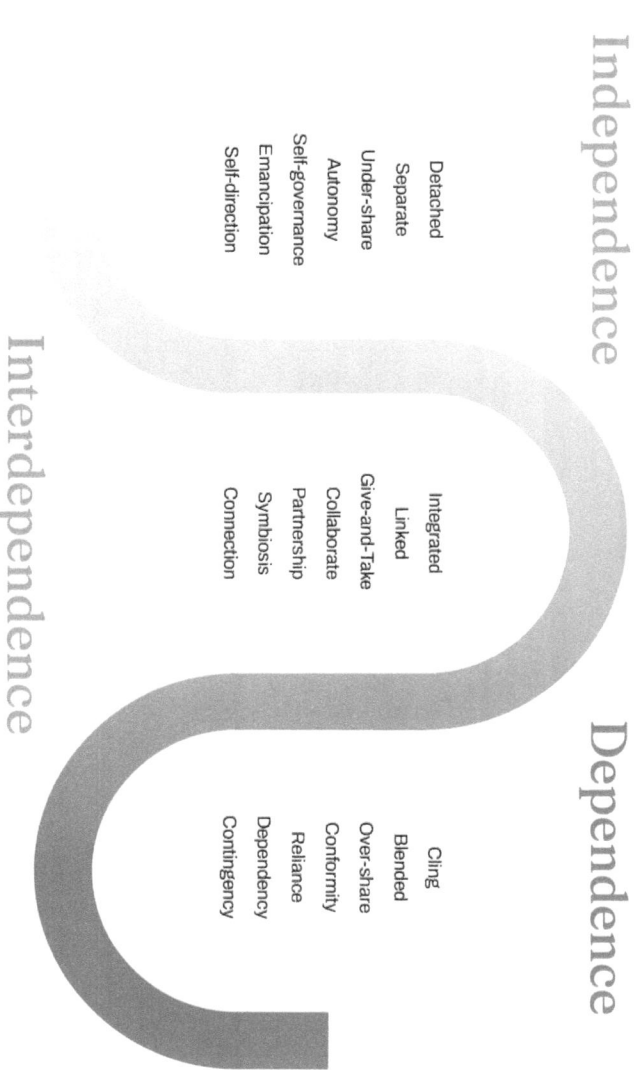

As you and your sibling build and strengthen your new relationship, you'll have to decide what interdependence looks like for you together, and what it looks like for you two within the context of your family of origin and your wider community. How much are you willing to give and share? What would you like to keep to yourself? Where do you see yourselves on the Holon Continuum?

CHAPTER 12

Conclusion

If you'd asked us what our goal was before we started this project, we probably would have told you it was to see each other as equals. We were ruled by competition as kids. We saw our different gifts and abilities as weapons we deployed against each other. Jessica's physical strength terrified Bluma, since she could use her hands and fists to pummel her. Bluma's verbal agility devastated Jessica, since she could arrange her words in such a way to make her feel like the smallest thing on the planet. This sense that we were such wildly different humans made us feel at odds with each other, and caused us to constantly compare ourselves in harmful ways. We were like battling superheroes in different colored capes, each drawing on a different arsenal of superpowers. In light of Jessica's dyslexia, Bluma's mastery of words and language fed into a superiority-inferiority complex. Jessica's being labeled the beautiful one, compared with Bluma's braininess, did too. We loved each other, but we saw each other as threats who continually caused real damage to our delicate and developing psyches.

So it seemed to make sense that repairing our sibling relationship would mean no longer seeing each other as competition, and instead as two human beings on equal footing.

Today, we know that's not true. Seeing each other as equals is not the goal. It's seeing each other, period.

Healing your adult sibling relationship means removing the prism of competition through which you used to see the world. It's about finally seeing your sibling for who they really are, unburdened by the toxic sibling rivalry that warped your perception for decades. It's about seeing your differences as precious and unique gifts that compliment each other and make you both more powerful together.

Processing our past through the six steps of our program, and then later, writing this book together, allowed us to see, with unparalleled clarity, the different talents and perspectives we both bring to the table. Bluma's deep understanding of human psychology and detail-oriented, rigorous research allowed us to build a novel and innovative program to heal our relationship. Jessica's entrepreneurial spirit and ability to see the big picture pushed us to think big, to think beyond ourselves, and to create a program not just for us, but for you, too.

Throughout this book, we've spoken at length about how healing our sibling relationship has restored a sense of balance in our lives. It's given us a presence of mind. It's not a magic wand that, badabing badaboom, will make all your troubles disappear. Nothing can do that. But it will give you a quiet inner strength to help you face them. Doing this work together restores your faith in yourself because you know, deeply and fully, that you are not alone. That the person closest to you in the world, who not only shares your DNA but knows you better than anyone else, is beside you on your journey through life, helping you through it.

We don't just mean this in a mystical sense. We mean this very seriously. For us, the proof is in this very book, the one you're holding in your hands right now.

Before we healed our relationship, never in a million years could we have imagined collaborating on a project, much less actually completing one, and successfully so. Writing a book about our sibling relationship, including our childhood memories, put our whole program to the test. Collaborating on a book is a difficult project to begin with. You have to meld your voices and agree on the substance and style and flow. In our case, we also had to agree on the stories we told. As you now know, the different ways we remembered the past was the very heart of so much of our discord. Our memories are different, since they're colored and shaped by our different experiences and emotional landscapes.

It took a lot of time and love and care to write this book together. It took patience to walk each other through our truths and see how they could be blended together. We needed to weave a new tapestry of stories that allowed us to move forward. And we did this during major turning points in our lives, and also during a wildly disrupting time in history: the Covid-19 pandemic. We were transitioning out of our married lives, and searched for a new direction that was supportive, grounding and encouraging. We found it in each other.

Creating this guide anchored us and pulled us into the future, one that is bright with hope and possibility. We are each other's north stars. It felt like reaching out to an extended hand pulling us toward what we were always meant to do. This book signifies the beginning of a new sibling relationship for us and for you. And, it's so much more than that. We hope this is the beginning of a society-wide transformation. A quiet revolution that will make all of our relationships kinder and truer.

If we heal ourselves, we can start taking the necessary steps to make sure the next generation of siblings is not burdened by the traumas and anxieties that plagued us, and pushed us to physically and emotionally abuse each other. We can end the cycle of violence. We want to help you heal your adult sibling relationship so that, together, we can pass it on for generations.

If family is the building block of society, ending sibling violence can be the first step toward ending violence on a larger scale.

We want to build a community of siblings with you and positively impact the world.

The research we've compiled, by luminaries like Drs. John and Julie Gottman, Laurie Kramer, Dan Siegel, C. Sue Carter, Stephen Porges, Dick Schwartz, Ronald Rohner, Frances Champagne, Wayne Dyer and Michell Brown, is a roadmap showing us what we need to know to become grounded and compassionate people with the skills to calmly and effectively address conflict. If we start now, and make sure the next generation of siblings are equipped with the necessary tool box, we can start effecting change on an unparalleled scale.

We want to start from the moment mothers conceive. When they go see their OBGYNs for their first scans, we want doctors to explain to them the effects stress can have on their developing babies and teach moms breathing and grounding exercises. We want moms to have access to support programs so that their in-utero babies develop as healthily as possible, and are primed to come into the world with the best neurological makeup to manage stress and conflict.

After babies are born, we want pediatricians to pick up the torch. We want them to be trained to explain to young parents how to nurture their babies so that they feel safe and loved, and continue to develop in ways that allow them to build healthy attachments with other people. This is especially important if and when parents have a second child. We want pediatricians to help parents learn how to bond with their new baby while making sure their other child continues to feel loved, seen and supported. This will ensure the parents help the new siblings adapt to rivalries, and encourage revelries, without having to compete for their parents' love and attention.

As kids grow up, we want parents and school teachers to teach them how to get along and resolve conflict, between siblings and, more broadly, with their classmates and other peers. Using resources like Laurie Kramer's, these adults can teach kids the skills they need to help them build positive, long-lasting relationships, including the foundational tenet of how to accept or decline an invitation to play.

As teenagers and adults who will fall in love and get into relationships, we want them to have access to therapists, clergy and coaches who will explain to them how their family relationships - with their parents and their siblings - affect how and who they choose as romantic partners.

As this support is provided, we want to collect data, boatloads of it, to analyze how all of these small changes affect human development. We want universities and institutions to get involved. As we were researching adult siblings and sibling dynamics for this book, there were numerous times we read research findings lamenting the fact that there were hardly any investigations or analyses on this subject. "Someone should be doing this," the authors would write.

We're going to do the research. And we want to do it with you.

By giving future generations of parents and siblings access to this kind of support and information, we are creating a new legacy for humanity. It will be a whole new way of living.

We want to change the world, and we want to change it with you. Join us.